WHY DO WE KILL?

WHY DO WE KILL?

THE PATHOLOGY
OF MURDER
IN BALTIMORE

By Kelvin Sewell
and Stephen Janis

Edited by
Alan Z. Forman

Co-Edited by Susan Older

BALTIMORE TRUE CRIME

Baltimore, MD / Publisher

Why Do We Kill?

Cover photos by Stephen Janis
Mugshots, courtesy BPD

This book is dedicated to Detectives Michael Moran, Joon Kim, Alan Dorsey, Juan Diaz, Terry Love Jr. and Napoleon McLain, who are the very fine men from the Baltimore City Police Department's Homicide Section that worked side by side with me 12 to 16 hours a day, year in year out solving murder cases.

Because of the severity of the homicide cases we were faced with on a daily basis, these fine men frequently had to put their own families second while favoring the families of homicide victims who desperately needed their support. Their dedication and loyalty helped to provide the families of murder victims with closure in their lives when we arrested the perpetrators who had killed their loved ones.

Guys, you've heard me say this a thousand of times before:

Thank you, and Good job!

I also want to dedicate this book to my three girls: To my wife Rhonda Sewell, who once stated, "The Police Department took my husband away from me years ago," and to my lovely daughters Ashley and Kandace Sewell who I am so proud of.

Thank you for being patient and staying close to each other while your husband and daddy was away for 22 years during my tour of duty with the BPD.

I love all of you so much.

Kelvin Sewell

CONTENTS

The Case Files

The Career Files

THE CASE FILES

FOREWORD

Why do we kill? It's the last question a homicide detective asks.

In a city like Baltimore which averages over 250 killings a year there's hardly time to think. Standing over a bullet-riddled body while a mother wails, speculation is a luxury.

Working eight cases at once — not uncommon in the Baltimore City Homicide Unit — Who cares? Is there a point at which a detective stops caring?

Chasing down prosecutors who don't feel like writing a warrant on Friday afternoon because it's 70 degrees outside and sunny, while you know that crucial piece of paper might take a killer off the streets for an entire weekend, doesn't leave you a lot of time to reflect.

Waking up and reading your name in the newspaper because of a feud between top prosecutors and the mayor, takes precedence over prosecuting a crooked cop. All you really want to do is leave it behind. You don't really want to know because in the end it's easier to keep your distance.

It's too easy to view the whole problem of violence as a matter of "us against them," of criminality versus law, of cop against killer.

We can just play into the media-wrought crime narrative, the nightly tales of random violence that suggest crime erupts with little rhyme or reason. And let the media feed the fear of criminal hoards knocking on the suburban door, ready to rob, steal, and kill without provocation.

Cops don't willingly take on the role of final buffer against murder and mayhem, the last line of defense against morally challenged thugs festering in ghettos largely of their own creation. It just happens. Then, somehow, we feel we have nothing to do with the mess. We're just the good guys.

I'm not saying we're not. I've watched police officers risk their lives in ways that are wholly selfless and remarkably courageous. But cops do what we're told. We are the instruments of politics, more now than ever.

However sometimes we have to step outside the box, so to speak. Give a clear view of the world as we see it. Deliver an honest dose of reality as real and unfiltered as a subjective observer's can be.

That's why I started this book, and why I begin with the question, fairly simple and yet ridiculously complex:

Why do we kill?

This is a question that goes to the root of why police exist at all, here as well as elsewhere, which is why I'm asking it. It asks why, in cities like Baltimore that spend a large portion of their budgets putting officers with guns into the neighborhoods and communities, do people continue to shoot and kill each other with reckless abandon?

Why, after spending millions of dollars on plainclothes units to disrupt drug dealers, using military-style tactics, does the shooting continue unabated?

These are questions that I want to answer because I think in the end it matters. We have to ask "Why?" We have to think. Because without asking "Why?" we may continue on the same path that has done little to improve the city where I was born, raised, and worked my entire life.

That's why the question is so important to me.

Because for all the money and time that's been poured into policing Baltimore, the city is truly no better off. Hundreds of people year in and year out pick up guns and try to kill each other. Largely because of this, 30,000 citizens moved out of Baltimore over the last decade, a period when the population of the State of Maryland grew by nine percent.

We've torn down housing projects and built new homes. Created empowerment zones and spent hundreds of millions to try and breathe new life into neighborhoods where much of the killing is done. We've paid more than three billion dollars over the past decade on direct costs alone for aggressive policing, arresting hundreds of thousands of poor, mostly black men and boys. Homicide detectives in Baltimore City have arrested hundreds of killers, even though, admittedly, our clearance rate could be a whole lot better.

Yet if I stood today on the corner of Preston and Greenmount, or Lombard and Carey, the Alameda and Belair, where we have concentrated those resources, I can tell you without question those neighborhoods and the people who still live there are no better off. They are not happier or safer. Instead, there is a sense of despair that has infected many parts of the city, a sense of hopelessness that I know has much to do with the reason people pick up a gun and aim it, with little provocation, at another human being.

Sure, the powers-that-be will tout statistics to prove me wrong. Numbers that show crime is down. Figures that paint an entirely different picture from what you will read in this book.

But this book isn't about numbers, it's about people.

It's about a little baby who spent only 44 days on Earth before his mother stuffed him down a hole in Druid Hill Park and left him for dead.

It's about a bear of a man who picked up a woman in a wheelchair and carried her across the room to witness how he had slit her daughter's throat, before stabbing her to death also.

It's about a woman so sure she was going to die at the hands of her abusive boyfriend that she sent herself a FedEx implicating him, that arrived the day we found her body decomposing on her couch.

This book is about people, because that's the part of the equation that the number-crunching just can't touch.

In big cities like Baltimore, statistics have taken over the human process of policing, and as a result, they hurt both cops and the very people they serve. During the city's experiment with "Zero Tolerance" policing, officers were judged by how many arrests they made — the more the better. Imagine the imperative: you were rewarded as a cop for the number of people you hauled off to jail. It didn't make a difference if the arrestee was a suspected murderer or someone drinking beer on their front stoop.

No one cared. It was all about the numbers — and numbers is what they got.

But nothing is more destructive to good policing and to the health of the community than unleashing the power to detain and arrest, to such unnecessary and ambiguous ends. Still, that's what has dominated our thinking for over a decade. It is at the core of our city's failure to truly make things better.

Because the fascination with numbers, and what they tell us about crime, continues to meddle in the discussion of what crime really is. Why do people break the law? Why do they kill?

I am not a criminologist per se, although I went to Coppin State University in Baltimore City and obtained a degree in criminology. The truth is I am a cop first, an officer who has worked Homicide, and also Narcotics and Internal Affairs, in one of the most complex police departments in the country.

So I'm not going to approach the question of why people do bad things, through the same filters as an academic or philosopher. Which doesn't mean I don't respect both professions. Because if there's one thing policing could use in this country, it's other perspectives outside of it.

My methodology is to start from the particular when delving into the seemingly aberrant behavior that has defined Baltimore for decades, spawning popular television shows like "The Wire" and "Homicide: Life on the Street." In other words, beginning with the cases I've worked. That is my reference point, the body on the street and all the chaos and corruption that surrounds it. From the details of these cases I hope to offer some perspective not just on the criminal mind, but the state of the community that has made violent death routine.

It's an approach I hope will shed some light on both human potentialities for bad behavior and what it means to be a cop who has to deal with that behavior regularly. It will offer some insight, I would hope, into what I believe is the pathology of murder in this city, and how it infects a community in death throes.

But what I hope most comes out in the words that follow is some sense of betterment that results from finally hearing the truth. That is, some sense of what really needs to be done to heal Baltimore from its state of pain, as told by a firsthand witness.

If anything positive results from my telling of these terrible stories of suffering, it will be a very real sense of what is happening on the streets. So far the truth has been too often papered over in a city that wants to overcome its violent reputation mostly by burying the dead-and-dying in a blanket of public relations spin.

I believe our strategy for curbing violence in Baltimore is wrong-headed. That we put too much emphasis after the fact, trying to solve complex problems with arrests, jail time, prisons and cops. That we have invested in the wrong ideas.

That's why I am asking the question, "Why Do We Kill?" Because what we're doing now is not working. As odd as that sounds coming from a former homicide detective, how do we know that what we're doing is right?

Let me tell you a story that will illustrate why I'm asking.

Much of my time as a homicide detective was spent in what is known as "the box." The room made famous in cop shows like "Homicide: Life on Street" and "The Wire." It's where we question both witnesses and suspects. On television the box is a scene of epic battles between cunning criminals and ingenious detectives. An OK Corral with a table and a couple chairs.

But in reality the box is a dull sort of social purgatory. More of a weigh station for the city's less fortunate and too-far-gone. Baltimore's version of a social terminus.

Truth be told, the cunning killers and edgy sociopaths of television rarely make an appearance in the room I work in. The visitors I encounter in the box are mostly young, often male. They are withdrawn and exhibit the natural defensiveness that comes with living in an economically deprived and by-default socially isolated ghetto.

But the point of the story and how it relates to the question of why we kill is pretty simple. So simple that it belies all the melodrama and posturing of television crime shows and nightly crime reports. It's a buzz-kill really for all the people who like to paint the misery of Baltimore as some sort of epic battle between good and evil, or incompetence and failed politics.

Here's how I know that whole big self-serving narrative is hot air.

So I'm in the box, sitting across from your average Baltimore killer. Or maybe he's just a thug with a "Money Over Bitches" tattoo inscribed around the back of his neck. Or maybe he's a knockoff Blood with an attitude that borders on autism.

Maybe he's sitting across from me acting like he's not scared. Like he doesn't want to talk because he's tough. Too tough. Or doesn't think I talked to his cohort just a few hours before, who gave me the whole story on how the young man sitting across from me pulled the trigger that shot the man who now lies on a gurney in the city morgue.

So let's just say I'm sitting across from this young man waiting for him to confess. Maybe he's got a record, maybe he says he wasn't in the neighborhood when the victim was shot. Maybe, too, he doesn't want to talk. Maybe he thinks I'll get tired.

We're at an impasse. He's slouching back in the chair. I'm asking questions that he's not answering, at least not truthfully. He's tough, stubborn; he's not afraid of me. So what do I do?

Get up in his face, scream obscenities, whoop and holler? Do I threaten him, glare at him like a maniac? Put my gun on the table? finger on the trigger?

Do I deny him food, play good cop bad cop like you see on television? The bad cop who has to be restrained?

Hell no, not even close.

I don't have to go that far to gain the upper hand, I have a secret weapon. A tactic I discovered that never fails to unnerve even the most stone cold Baltimore thugs. A counterattack that leaves them speechless. A foil that has delivered a psychological advantage to me in countless interviews over dozens of cases.

"If you're so tough," I say, "recite the alphabet."

The challenge hits them like a ringer. It stuns them.

Usually it's the first query in the entire interview that even elicits a response. A challenge that results in a "what the fuck?" look that prompts a deeper slump into their chair. Sometimes they get angry. Not an obvious anger, but an indignant guffaw. A roll of the eyes. A snicker.

Then they try. And I wait.

And of all the dozens of young people I've sat across from, not a single suspect or hardened thug has been able to do it. Complete the alphabet? Not one.

Not one.

I don't let them mumble through the L-M-N-O-P part either, which they often try to do. I make them speak clearly. I make them say each and every letter. And to a person, they cannot.

They couldn't do it if their lives depended on it, if I told them they could go free right then and there. Even if I offered them straight-up immunity (which I couldn't), they could not string together the 26 letters that comprise the English language.

With this in mind, let me ask the question again: *Why do we kill?*

Well, killing is of course innate. We're all capable of it. A skill buried in our subconscious but very much present. A behavior that a cop learns quite quickly is not as unusual as one might think.

But in Baltimore that ability goes beyond logic or reason. People kill because they're angry over a slight. Frustrated over a hard look. Pissed off because somebody talked to their girl. They kill and are killed for nothing.

Bear in mind that the more than 200 people killed on-average annually in Baltimore are the successful homicides. Every year there are over 600 shootings — what we call failed homicides; then there are thousands of assaults and beatings, knife fights and fistfights, and even vehicular killings and strangulations that are not recorded as homicides.

So when I think about the question of why we kill, I think about the alphabet, and what it means. Because some say the cause is our faulty education system. Some people attribute it to a lack of interest in learning, an antipathy to knowledge. Others attribute it to broken homes, lack of parenting, and a failure of communal guidance.

But I look at the failure to know the letters of the English language from a different angle. I look at it as recognition of reality. A sign of despair, a psychic sickness that is fostered by the crumbling row homes along the broken sidewalks of Baltimore neighborhoods. I see it as a sort of recognition of the blindness that afflicts the city.

Isn't it a reflection of a world that is poor, neglected and only knows governance in the form of punishment? I look at it the same way I do when I drive down Route 83 on the JFX and see a prison complex bigger than any factory or office building in the city. I see it as the mirror image of a city that suffers from terminal despair, where there is indeed no social compact.

Maybe I'm overcomplicating it? Maybe I'm giving people who are often described as "knuckleheads" too much credit? In fact, maybe it just doesn't matter? After all, most city cops live in suburbs far removed from the mayhem and the violence that afflicts Baltimore. Maybe it's the cops, who are disconnected and just don't understand?

But I think the question is worth considering, given that violence in this city has not stopped.

I grew up in Baltimore; it was my home. I spent 22 years of my life trying to make it better. It didn't work. So I'm sharing what I've seen and what I know that might help change that. Or at least add a meaningful set of facts to the debate. Think of it as evidence that can be used to indict the city for what it lacks, or maybe give some thought to what it really needs. We may never understand all the different factors that went into creating the environment that makes Baltimore so deadly. We might not even agree on just one.

Sometimes I've thought it would have been better just to start over in Baltimore. Somehow go back and reset the whole thing. Try to stop the jobs from leaving, the factories from closing, the prison from being expanded and the Police Department from becoming infused with politics. But that's not possible. All we can do now is try to mitigate the pain by looking at the city with honest eyes.

Because murders radiate pain. Sudden and violent death moves like a wave through the community left behind. Each victim leaves a hole in a loved one's heart. Whether it's a drug dealer with a lifelong criminal record or a city councilman like Ken Harris, who was murdered during a botched robbery, the bullet leaves its mark on everyone.

I hope by recounting these cases, and in parts of this book my experience as an officer, I can infuse the debate over crime and violence with realism. Nothing has made the situation worse in Baltimore than the attempt to downplay the severity of the problem.

The constant pressure to underreport crime. The need to paper-over the suffering on the East and West Sides of the city so the Inner Harbor can continue to attract tourists, and neighborhoods like Federal Hill and Canton can continue thriving.

The problem is, you can't contain it. Crime always seeps through the boundaries, and along with it, suffering. Pretending like it isn't happening has little effect on the steady drumbeat of death. In fact, many times the cover-up is worse than the crime. A dose of honesty and realism might give us the sense to figure out what is and is not working. Otherwise, without the truth, we are simply blind.

So as you read this book, bear in mind that it's not intended to be simply a "tell all" or a series of revelations about crime and criminals. Instead, I hope the cases I write about and the experiences I share will become one piece that will help solve the puzzle of why Baltimore has such a penchant for violence.

And maybe give insight into what makes killing in this city different from why it occurs in other places.

Maybe it will, maybe it won't. But it's the least I could do for the people of the City of Baltimore that I love.

CASE FILE 1

The Bounty Hunters

Anthony Williams, a/k/a Antmo

"Why do we kill?"

The question hit me as I watched a homicide suspect named Antmo light a match.

We were standing on the roof outside the Baltimore City Homicide floor on a cold winter night. Antmo was taking a smoke break.

He lit the cigarette deliberately, almost too carefully. He took a deep drag and inhaled. And that's when I wondered about why people kill. I wondered as I watched Antmo.

It's a question a homicide detective rarely asks. "Why?" is kind of a luxury.

We want to know "How" so we can figure out "Who."

But as Anthony Williams, a/k/a Antmo, focused on enjoying his cigarette, the question seemed appropriately timed.

We had just finished questioning Antmo about the death of Petro Taylor. Antmo had said nothing.

He was a short, muscled punk. Even though we already knew what he'd done, he sat there with a thousand yard stare.

But as his cigarette dragged down to the butt, I suggested Antmo put it out with his fingers. I don't know why I said it. Probably anger, frustration. Needless to say he wasn't interested.

"Yo man, I'd burn myself," he protested.

"Well how do you think Petro felt when you lit the match?"

Antmo turned to Detective Mike Moran.

"I don't think Sergeant Sewell likes me."

Detective Moran shrugged.

"No, he doesn't."

And that's when it dawned on me. That's when I posed the question, and hit upon a theory.

You see, we knew Antmo lit the match that set fellow gang member Petro Taylor on fire. Yet he didn't seem to grasp what I was saying. The discomfort of the glowing ember that would burn his hand, juxtaposed with the horrific pain of being engulfed in flames until you die was apparently beyond his comprehension.

With all the killers I'd sat across the table from, listening to them lie or confess, it was this inexplicable disconnect of Antmo that they all had in common. A lack of empathy that leads me to conclude that murder in Baltimore is pathological.

Did he not understand that the tiny pain he might have felt was simply a glimpse of the excruciating suffering that Petro experienced before he died in a ball of flames? Was Antmo that disconnected and unaware? Or had the hopelessness that pervades this town infected its social fabric to a degree that killers like Antmo are just a product of the landscape — born to one day walk through the doors of my office?

Let me elaborate.

If you visit Baltimore, drive to the northwest section of the city. I recommend Reisterstown Road.

It's an old commercial thoroughfare offering uneven sidewalks lined with chicken shacks, liquor stores, nail shops, gas stations and no shortage of empty storefronts. One endless colorless mile after another as if washed in silt.

It's like the ghetto without the dramatic urban decay that you find in the heart of a once thriving city. Reisterstown Road is just a static strip of hopelessness.

A few blocks past Northern Parkway look to your left.

There you'll see a Red Carpet Inn. A pretty grim structure. A low-slung building that looks more like a prison than a motel.

If you're really curious, venture up a caged stairwell on the left side of the motel. Third floor, take another left and walk about 50 feet. You should be standing in front of Room 312.

That's the room where it happened. The case that taught me that murder in Baltimore is pathology, not an illness or disease, but a sort of unspoken war against life. Why it grows, how it evolves.

In that room one night in December 2008 there was a murder. Not a simple murder. Not one man kills another, or jealous lover slays a rival.

This murder was carried out in a series of concerted actions by no less than eight teenagers, and, for all intents and purposes, a few children.

It involved a beating, a stabbing, and burning a man alive. A gruesome series of violent acts that speak to real violence beneath the somber guise of the disjointed strip-mall-rolled-into-decay that is Northwest Baltimore.

It was the night a young man named Petro Taylor would suffer a brutal, painful, and ignominious death.

And it all started with a party.

Members of a Baltimore gang known as the Bounty Hunters had gathered at the Red Carpet Inn to drink, and to have sex.

Technically the Bounty Hunters are part of the Bloods, the de facto collection arm of one of the nation's most notorious street gangs.

But gangs in Baltimore tend to be the equivalent of brand name knockoffs, and Baltimore's version of the Bounty Hunters was no exception.

The Baltimore Bounty Hunters were not tied to the Bloods officially, just a nomenclature adopted by a collection of thugs who had big aspirations but little guile.

This doesn't mean they weren't dangerous, in fact their lack of centralized command and haphazard operational strategy makes them an unwieldy and unpredictable threat.

One of the organizers of the party, a 27-year-old "original gangster" (OG) who has been around, told me during my investigation he and several other older gang members had organized the get-together to sleep with the gang's nubile females, some as young as 16.

They had purchased several bottles of Ciroc, the vodka made from grapes promoted by Sean "Diddy" Combs (originally known as "Puff Daddy" and later "P.Diddy) in honor of President Barack Obama.

They rented Room 312, and had planned to conduct their version of a Northwest Baltimore orgy.

The so-called women gang members were really children. Girls the age of my daughters, young teens who willingly congregated in a seedy motel room to be plied with vodka in exchange for sex.

Sometime during the party Petro Taylor showed up, a short, skinny 20-year-old with a healthy rap sheet and a name that foreshadowed what was about to befall him that night.

Petro was a high school dropout and a petty drug dealer.

But he also had a serious problem.

Petro had been given $200 cash to put in the commissary account of the gang's original gangster. The OG was locked up in Baltimore County for attempted murder.

Anyone who knows prison understands how important commissary money is. It buys the niceties, gum or a comb, things we take for granted in the free world. It also buys the narcotics.

However for reasons we will never know, Petro never delivered the cash.

So when Petro arrived at the motel, a gang member named Terrell Gray confronted him about it. But Petro gave him lip, and a fight ensued.

To this day I don't know if they planned to kill Petro from the outset, but they certainly had intent to do serious harm.

After Gray and Petro finished fighting, Gray left the party. He said later that he was done with the gang, and had left the party on purpose.

But Petro kept mouthing off and the fighting resumed.

During this go-round almost all the other gang members joined in.

Within seconds Petro was surrounded by nearly a dozen men, boys, and, yes, girls. He was beaten nearly unconscious as other gang members looked on, sipping vodka commemorating the country's first African-American president, from paper cups.

When the beating was over, Petro lay semi-conscious on a bed, bleeding from multiple wounds to his face.

He was still alive in fact. I can't be sure but it seems, based on what we learned later from the medical examiner, had they simply left him there, or dropped him off at a hospital he would have been up and about the next day.

But as Petro lay on the bed, several of the gang members hatched a plan, a plan that turned into a prolonged and painful death sentence for Petro.

I can't really speculate on how this plan was hatched or who thought it up. My assumption is that it was Antmo. He was the true stone cold killer, a hardened street thug who had killed before.

But even if it was Antmo who proscribed the events I am about to recount, I still to this day struggle with it.

It's one thing to say we all have the capacity to kill, that it's innate. If someone attacks you, threatens the life of your child, for example, you have the ability to respond, believe me.

But to contemplate someone's death, to stand around in a motel room and figure out how you're going to finish off a man who is still alive and breathing, that's a different story. That's the work of a killer.

Killers are a different breed. They're not the imaginative and diabolical criminals that populate crime shows. What sets them apart is simply the fact that, for whatever reason, they have no empathy.

Some would call this being a sociopath. But that's embellishing.

The Baltimore killer is straightforward, no-nonsense, down to business — if not sloppy and stupid and so utterly detached and comfortable with murder, if you spend enough time with him it indeed begins to seem routine.

How such people get there is the important question. Why is it common to Baltimore? How can such a small city produce the Bounty Hunters, child killer Melvin Jones, and even 14-year-old murderer Devon Richardson in a span of only several years? That's where the pathology comes into play, or maybe we should call it a communal virus, a social pathogen.

But back to Room 312.

While Petro lay on the bed half conscious, probably moaning in pain, someone came up with the idea to put him in the trunk of a car and drive him to Leakin Park.

But here's where the story takes a surreal twist.

Before they actually moved him, someone had the semi-bright idea of wrapping Petro in a motel blanket. Even odder, a young college girl named Tanisha Lawson took a sheet and shower curtain, a pillowcase, the motel phone, and a remote control.

Next, as they carried Petro down the stairs before placing him in the trunk of a car, the suspects made sure they did so in full view of the security cameras. In fact one of our first witnesses was able to identify almost all the culprits from that footage.

And this is where the tale turns even more bizarre. The driver, Tanisha Lawson, the petite child with a cursive smile, backs her car up next to the stairwell, gets out and opens the trunk.

Murder One.

I remember interviewing Tanisha, sitting in the box watching her as she calmly related the story of what happened next. I even remember trying to help her, trying to give her a bit of an out for Murder One with intent.

"So you popped the trunk from inside the car, right?" I questioned, offering her a little wiggle room. Maybe she didn't know they were putting Petro in the trunk?

"No," she said without flinching. "The latch was broken so I had to get out of the car."

It gets worse.

With Petro in the trunk, Antmo in the front seat, and Sierra Pyle and Greshauna Rogers in the back, and Tanisha driving, the gang members didn't have a concrete plan.

For a while they simply drove around, unsure of what to do. Petro was still alive. They could hear him moaning from the trunk.

So, Antmo came up with an idea, take him to Leakin Park and burn him.

Leakin Park is Baltimore's ad hoc cemetery. It's the body dumping ground of first resort. Once Antmo came up with the idea, not a single one of the girls objected. No one said a word in protest. They admitted as much in their confessions.

"Burn him," I remember Tanisha saying when I asked her what they planned to do with him after he was placed in the trunk of her car.

"You didn't know when you were driving around what you were going to do with Petro?" I asked her.

"Yes, I did," she repeated. "We were going to burn him."

Tanisha then drove to a gas station on Reisterstown Road. There she bought a two-liter bottle of Pepsi. But it wasn't because she was thirsty.

"I drank some and then I filled it with gasoline," she confessed.

With the two liters of gasoline in the empty soda bottle, the group proceeded to Leakin Park.

And that's when things become inexplicable.

Petro was hardly dead, and all the passengers in that car could hear it. He was moaning in pain, breathing heavily. It was like a scene out of "Goodfellas" when the gangster they thought they had killed started kicking the trunk, but instead of Joe Pesci and Robert

DeNiro, you have a bunch of tiny teenage girls.

When they finally arrived at the utility road next to a stream deep inside Leakin Park, Antmo and 16-year-old Greshauna Rogers got out of the car, opened the trunk, and together they stabbed Petro 22 times.

Then the group moved Petro from the car to a small patch of forest adjacent to the stream. There the girls laid out a pillow and blanket for him. They placed him on the ground and Tanisha poured the gasoline from the soda bottle, dousing Petro with accelerant.

Finally, Antmo took out a book of matches. The girls told me he lit the match, held it high in the air, then dropped it on Petro's body, which burst into flames. During Petro's autopsy the medical examiner found leaves in his lungs. Petro was alive when Antmo lit that match. These three girls and a second-rate thug had actually burned a man alive.

The next day a park employee spotted the smoldering body.

When we arrived he was half cremated. The ashes of his body were spread across the leaves like a soot blanket. The stench from the summary execution by burning was lingering and putrid.

Immediately we had the lead they left us. My detective Mike Moran found the phone, the television remote and the blankets. All the items were traceable back to the Red Carpet Inn.

At the motel we confiscated the security camera tapes. We also were able to trace back the items left at the park to Room 312. But when we called the crime lab and informed management that we would be conducting forensics in the room, we made another grisly discovery.

The room had been rented.

Two poor tourists had slept on the bed that underneath the sheets was covered with blood just one night after Petro had lain there half-conscious and beaten.

Why the motel maids didn't report the bed's being soaked with blood is an open question. Perhaps they never removed the bedspread when they tidied up the room and got it ready for the next rental?

However the tapes from the security cameras and the registration information were all we needed. Most of the gang members had literally mugged for the camera.

We had plenty.

In the meantime the ME finished the autopsy and delivered grim results.

Petro's death was the result of multiple causes. Blunt force trauma to the head, stab wounds to the chest, arms, neck and head. And finally, smoke inhalation.

Petro was breathing when his body was doused with gasoline and set on fire. He was burned alive.

I can only hope for his sake he was unconscious.

The tapes from the security cameras were like watching a custom-made movie of the crime, left like a gift for homicide detectives.

First we had a tape of one suspect checking into the motel. Then a shot of a large group leaving the room after the fight, we believed.

Then we had footage of the suspects carrying the blanket, pillowcases, and other evidence out of the room.

And finally, we actually had a clear shot of several of the gang members carrying Petro's body to the car. It was unbelievable, these kids were that stupid. Of course, what they lacked in criminal intelligence they made up for in pure ruthlessness.

Our next big break came when Detective Moran located one of the men captured on the video. For his protection I will not reveal his identity, but needless to say he gave us the name of almost every suspect caught on film.

Still, we needed someone to piece together for us who did what and when.

And that person turned out to be another member of the Bounty

Hunters who wasn't too thrilled with gang life. He was there for the fight but had left shortly after Petro was knocked unconscious. But he also knew who stayed behind in the motel room.

I remember as he ticked off the nicknames and we started piecing together who did what. That's when things got unsettling.

For other than Anthony Williams a/k/a Antmo, the three primary actors who carried out the execution of Petro Taylor were the young women I mentioned before: Tanisha Lawson, Greshauna Rogers, and Sierra Pyle, who had just turned 20.

These weren't tough-looking amazons. These were petite girls.

And so for the next several weeks we brought each girl in for questioning, and as we did, my thoughts always strayed back to "Why?"

Greshauna Rogers was only 16, a short plump girl from Northwest Baltimore. She not only confessed to beating up Petro in the motel, but later stabbing him multiple times as he lay in the trunk prior to being burned.

Sierra Pyle admitted to carrying the evidence out of the motel room and helping to carry his body to the spot in the woods where he was eventually lit on fire.

Still, the most troubling of the three female accomplices was perhaps Tanisha Lawson.

A petite, unassuming girl, and as I said before, quiet and cold in the box.

Yet it didn't take much to get her to talk either. Once we told her what we had, she simply recounted the tale and her role in Petro's death as matter-of-fact as if she were telling a girlfriend how she got lost en route to a party.

Her voice was steady, her tone even and unemotional. Her gaze was unflinching.

It was her car, as I said before, that delivered Petro to the park.

It was she who purchased the soda bottle and filled it with gasoline, then poured it on the sheets and pillowcases before laying Petro out in the park to die.

This small diminutive college girl even took part in the beating.

And so she sat, not a single moment of body language that implied fear, not one tear of remorse, not even the quiver in the voice of a person who has a semblance of conscience.

Instead, Tanisha simply sat there and talked about how she planned, participated in, and later covered up the drawn-out execution of Petro Taylor.

I'll never forget when I asked her, "Why?"

"Because that's what we were told to do," she said.

The gang was more powerful than the family, enabling a child to commit a horrific murder.

And with Tanisha's confession I had come full circle to the question prompted by Antmo's callousness.

For she wasn't a child of the ghetto, a castaway without parental guidance or educational opportunity. She didn't fit the mold.

I remember calling Tanisha's mother shortly after she confessed.

"Your daughter is here with us at Homicide," I said.

"That's impossible, she's in Atlanta."

"Ma'am, you need to pull over," I said before handing the phone to Tanisha.

Without missing a beat, Tanisha picked up the phone.

"Mom we're here because we killed someone."

Then all I could hear was her mother screaming, a mother I would later learn took her daughter to church every Sunday. A woman who worked her way up as a regional manager of a fast-food company so her daughter could attend college in Atlanta. A mother who cared so much for her daughter she still refused to believe, even after Tanisha confessed, that her little girl poured gasoline over the body of Petro Taylor.

A woman whose only mistake may have been trying to raise her daughter in Baltimore.

Which brings me back to that night standing outside of Homicide with Antmo.

Antmo, the big bad killer who nonchalantly dropped the match on the body of his friend but who didn't want to feel the fleeting pain of a lit cigarette butt. The man whose ruthless stupid idea to kill Petro led to seven of his fellow gang members' serving out jail sentences ranging from three years for the men who initiated the fight, to 20 years for each of the girls.

Ruined lives; a dead young man.

All I was left with was this thought: Was Antmo really a stone cold killer?

Or was he just an idiot, a product of despair? Someone so stupid and yet so ruthless that only a town with an irreparably broken heart could stand him?

A town with a disease called Murder.

CASE FILE 2

MELVIN JONES

Melvin Jones

The strange thing about being a homicide detective is that you can taste death before you smell it.

I mean, you've smelled it so many times, where bodies decompose and cook on hot summer nights, festering in the basements of vacant row homes and stuffed inside the trunks of abandoned cars, left to rot for days. You smell it, too, downstairs in the city morgue where corpses lie in neat rows outside the autopsy room after a weekend of bloodshed.

And in the humid air of a hot summer day in Baltimore.

To a certain extent you get used to it.

Yes. And after awhile, after you get too used to it, you can taste it, sense its arrival in the air before the real stench hits you in the face. That's because death isn't just an odor, it's an admixture of rotted flesh and rapid decay, nature's best way of saying stay away. It's a warning. And believe me, it works.

So on that summer morning in July of 2006, when I started to walk down the wooded path behind a church on the East Side near Belair Road, I knew a dead body was not far away.

And this time, it was the body of a child.

I remember following the dirt byway behind a convenience store where 11-year-old Irvin Harris was last seen alive. That's when the dread began. Nobody likes to find the body of a kid.

It didn't take long to locate his remains up a small hill, lodged beneath a tree.

There, lying in woods like a broken doll was Irvin, on his back, dead. The body was partially decomposed. He was naked from the waist up. Animals had eaten off a good chunk of his face.

There were puncture wounds across his chest, cuts with distinct slashing marks on his still-tiny hands. The boy, as young as he was, had put up a fight.

We already knew who killed him. Who murdered Irvin was not a mystery. In fact, the reason for writing about this case, like others in this book, is not because it entails some sort of convoluted mystery. Instead, there is something more important to be learned, or perhaps just acknowledged about how people die in Baltimore. Something about how human beings respond to extreme situations worth recognizing, about the consequences of neglect worth comprehending.

When the boy disappeared, his sister told detectives from the Missing Persons Bureau a family friend named Melvin Jones had told her he "hurt the boy."

Melvin had been the boy's so-called babysitter, a 52-year old former sex offender who watched the boy after school while his mother got high on dope.

Melvin was seen leaving the convenience store with Irvin just hours before the boy disappeared.

So we got a warrant, and the search began.

Melvin wasn't hard to find. He'd been riding Baltimore's version of a subway — a one-line ride to futility that travels between a suburb called Owings Mills and Johns Hopkins Hospital — all day. When he finally got hungry and decided to stop at a McDonald's, a patrol officer spotted him and made the arrest.

I wasn't quite prepared for what I saw when Melvin was escorted into our offices. I knew he would be more than a little off; after all, he previously pled guilty to sexually abusing a young boy in 2002.

But when he was walked through the Homicide floor and dropped inside the box, it took me awhile just to take in all the utter strangeness of the man sitting alone on a chair fidgeting like a child.

He didn't look like a thug.

He sat up straight, not the usual ghetto slouch. He was wearing a white pullover shirt with a flounced collar, not the typical gear for a West Baltimore man in his fifties.

He was thin as a rail, and looked too well put together. Truthfully I didn't know how he managed to survive in a neighborhood riddled with Bloods and Crips, who typically wear galaxy-sized T-shirts and pants with the waist down at their knees.

But there was something else about him. The way he held his head up like a hen, a matronly guise, or some sort of odd-minded delusion.

We already had a Murder One warrant for Melvin, and the State's Attorney's Office was prepared to bring the case before the grand jury for first-degree murder.

The case had attracted a lot of media attention. A missing child, a suspect who was already a sex offender, the last thing we wanted was to show up in court with a circumstantial case that could easily be picked apart by a good defense attorney.

So even though we were dead tired, we decided to interrogate him and get a confession.

Melvin was detached and defiant at first. Detective Bob Cherry handled the questioning.

Since the case had been a high priority, none of us had slept for almost 36 hours. Detective Cherry was trying to guilt Jones into confessing.

Earlier in the day we had served a search and seizure warrant at Jones's apartment. The place was immaculately clean, like it had just been scrubbed over by a forensics team.

But inside a trash can we found bits of papers torn into shreds.

Irvin's name was written on several scraps. When it was assembled, it appeared to be the remains of a love letter from Melvin to Irvin.

So with the evidence from Melvin's house and a statement from Irvin's sister, Cherry continued to press Melvin.

"What you did was sick, sick," Cherry said to Jones. "Just tell us, we already know."

But Melvin wasn't budging.

Tired, near exhausted, I joined Cherry in the box. Truthfully, for the first several minutes I nearly fell asleep.

But after ten minutes of listening to Detective Cherry and Jones go back and forth, I finally lost my patience.

As I've said many times, I learned long ago that you don't get far by haranguing a suspect. It just doesn't work. The suspect has the right to remain silent. If you push too far, they'll simply lawyer up.

But that night, I was tired, dead tired. And Melvin was getting on my nerves.

So I sat up, leaned across the table, and said as loud as I could: "Look Melvin, you did it, we know you did it, everyone knows you did it, so you might as well tell us now rather than later. Then we can all get some sleep."

And, to our surprise, Melvin shrugged and said nonchalantly, "Okay, I'll tell you."

And with that, he did.

The first thing Melvin wanted us to know, was that little Irvin, the child whose body we found just hours earlier rotting in the woods, was gay.

"Oh, he was gay," Melvin said.

"You're telling me an 11-year-old boy was gay?" I asked.

"Oh yes, he was gay, believe me," he said, rolling his eyes.

According to Melvin, he and Irvin were in love. An intense love, Melvin claimed, a bond that had developed over several years, since the boy was nine.

Alone with the boy while his mother was getting high, Melvin would take Irvin back to his house after school where they would have sex regularly. An ongoing abuse that had lasted for at least a year.

But trouble began, Melvin said, when Irvin called him and asked for money.

Melvin said he was already suspicious that Irvin was "seeing" someone else, so when Irvin asked for cash, he told us he knew the little boy was up to something.

"What for?" Melvin recalled asking Irvin. "I want to buy this girl a present," Irvin said.

The present turned out to be a teddy bear with Irvin's name on it.

The girl's name? "Jessica," Melvin said derisively, a dismissive tone toward Irvin that he would maintain throughout the confession.

The fact that Irvin was interested in another person, let alone a girl, was too much for Melvin. It was a violation of his trust. A disrespect of their bond, of their so-called love, he told us.

"One of them was going to die," Melvin said. "It just depended on who I found first."

Now I can't explain to you, or even make sense of a man like Melvin. You'd have to sit there in the chair in front of him just to get an idea of how screwed up he really was. But let me try.

Imagine if you had killed someone. Imagine too, if it had been a child. How would you feel?

Would you sit in front of two homicide detectives, talking casually about your misdeeds like a trip to the beach? Would you speak defiantly about a little boy's sexuality and actions as if somehow the child was responsible for what you did?

Probably not.

But that's just what Melvin did.

It turned out that Melvin found Irvin first. He told us he asked the boy to accompany him to a corner store in the neighborhood, having already decided to kill him.

On the way home, Melvin suggested they take a short cut through the woods. In a wooded area behind the church he pulled out a knife and started stabbing the child, 14 times in all.

But Irvin fought back, Melvin told us. The little boy raised his hands to deflect the knife, scrambling to get away. And then Melvin shared a detail of the murder that still haunts me. He said that as he was thrusting the knife into the boy's chest, Irvin put up his hands.

"But Melvin, you know I love you," he supposedly pleaded.

Needless to say there were at least half a dozen cuts on the boy's hands, defensive wounds that prove at least Irvin tried to deflect the deadly thrusts of Melvin's knife.

Melvin kept on stabbing the child even as he begged for his life. All the while Melvin telling us how little Irvin deserved it because he had been unfaithful.

I remember sitting there while Melvin told us this story. His manner was calm, almost detached. Like he was telling a friend about a spat with a girlfriend over a cup of coffee.

Then, when it seemed Melvin had finished and we were about to turn off the tape, he surprised us.

"You've been so nice to me," he said, hesitating, "I'm going to show you were I hid the knife."

A confession — and the murder weapon. This case is over, I remember thinking.

Driving to the address where Melvin said he hid the knife, I could hear him muttering to himself in the back seat of the car.

"He had a girlfriend, huh," he was saying with disdain. "He had a girlfriend," he kept repeating with a touch of what seemed like sarcasm.

I asked him, "Is that why you killed him? Melvin, is that what set you off?"

"Yeah, he said. Then repeated, "He had a girlfriend," in the same nasty, dismissive tone.

When we arrived at a manhole roughly 10 blocks south of where Irvin's body was found, Melvin was silent as we slipped back the steel cover. Sitting to the side of a runoff drain was what looked like a carving knife, maybe 14 inches long, covered in blood.

Then he showed us where he hid his own bloodied T-shirt. After he killed Irvin he had also taken off the boy's clothes and tossed them back in the woods not far from the body. Half naked, he pulled some pants and a shirt off a neighborhood clothesline.

When we returned to Homicide, Melvin said he was hungry. He looked unfazed, not even tired.

One of the rules we have in Homicide, is that we always give suspects whatever they want to eat. We don't deny anything, unlike what you see on television where the suspects sit in the box sweating, asking for a cup of coffee or a glass of water. That never happens. It would be stupid and shortsighted, handing a defense attorney an easy ploy for the jury to say we coerced a confession.

Stone cold killers like Melvin get hungry. He wanted a sub, as I recall.

So one of the detectives went to Subway and picked up a sandwich. I remember watching him eat, sitting in one of the cells in the back of the Homicide floor where we hold suspects. He just sat there eating. Not a care in the world. Like he had just applied for a driver's license. Eating a meal as if nothing had happened.

After Melvin's confession, the case hit the media like wildfire. There was a furor over the fact that the mother had allowed Jones access to her son.

But it gets worse.

It turns out that Melvin had been allowed to pick up Irvin at the Collington Elementary School. Worse yet, he was a designated family representative, meaning he was allowed inside the school and of course, near other children.

One of the staff members at the school found Melvin on the state's Sex Offender Registry and banned him. The school official even warned Irvin's mother, Shandra Harris.

But Shandra Harris had her own problems. She was a heroin addict with a rap sheet. Who knows what really went on, who knows why she let Melvin near her son? But you can imagine how little parenting an unemployed heroin addict is capable of doing.

Eventually charges of child abuse and neglect were filed against her. She copped a plea and served six months in jail.

I never saw Melvin again after his meal in prison. He pled guilty to murdering Irvin and received a life sentence.

But his demeanor and attitude about the killing stuck with me, as does the behavior of suspects in many of my cases.

In his mind, I believe he truly thought the child had betrayed him. To him, the killing was justified.

Plus it wasn't like Melvin had never done this before. In 2002 he was convicted of abusing another boy, a 13-year-old whom he invited into the home he shared with his mother. They had sex and he was charged with sex offense and rape. But Melvin claimed then too that it was consensual.

He told police back then he was a "borderline pedophile" who needed help. And yet nothing was done.

By the time Melvin met Irvin Harris in 2004, I'm sure the pathology had set in, assuring him that what he was doing was okay.

Still, the fact that Melvin Jones could walk the streets, the fact that someone who had been accused of touching a four-year old girl when he was 16 but never charged was given access to a nine-year-old boy says something about the world of poverty and dysfunction in Baltimore.

It goes deeper than politics, it goes deeper than criminality.

It's more comparable to a cancer, this social pathology. The immune system of the community has been compromised to such a degree that it took decades to finally put Melvin where he belonged, and by then it was too late.

Irvin Harris was already dead.

CASE FILE 3

DEVON RICHARDSON

Devon Richardson

Take my advice, skip cop shows.

I do.

They're a waste of time, based on false assumptions. And even when they borrow from reality, like "The Wire," they miss the mark. This isn't the opinion of a cynical cop. Or even an attempt to parse what's authentic and what's not.

Truthfully, cop shows aren't meant to give us a measured dose of realism, or even a balanced sense of what life is like on the streets of Baltimore. They're not lenses through which we see the truths of poverty and injustice.

Cop shows, put simply, are created to give us a pass we don't deserve. They're just a cheap way of granting the audience a pardon.

They play out scenarios that don't exist, like the good but flawed cop who is thwarted by the bad but ambitious cop in pursuit of the consummate bad guy.

It's dishonest, Disney-type stuff.

The real story of Baltimore, the real confluence of poverty, violence, and enforcement is awash in an ocean of entrenched neglect, neglect in which we all share a part.

Cop shows are just a way of pointing the finger at someone else. Even "The Wire" is, at its best, a collective, albeit sophisticated forbearance for a loan we've all taken out but refuse to pay.

How did I come to this conclusion?

Through cases, murder cases. By witnessing how people really die, and why.

Or, in one case, simply from the words spoken by a child.

"I bet you can't shoot that lady."

"What did you say?" I asked the suspect.

"Derrius said, 'I bet you can't shoot that lady,' but we didn't think he would do it."

Maybe it was a dare, or a joke? Or one of those stupid thought-less things uttered by teenagers... in Baltimore. He didn't elaborate.

But those words, spoken in a dusty alley on a hot September afternoon in 2007, were a fitful death sentence for 67-year-old Janice Letmate. A death sentence that intertwined several lives in what could best be called the "dance of grays" — the small permutations of choice and circumstance that invariably decide who lives and dies in Baltimore City.

When I'm done, you tell me who's at fault, you tell me where the grays become black and white so that the case makes sense.

Ms. Letmate had just gotten off the bus near her East Baltimore row home. She worked at a downtown law firm. A dutiful legal secre-tary, a mother and a grandmother, a stubborn widow who refused to move from her lifelong home even though her children fretted as the neighborhood sank into the perfect Baltimore malaise of small-time drug dealing and itinerant Section 8-fueled despair.

That same afternoon 14-year-old Devon Richardson was stand-ing in an alley holding a .22-caliber shotgun. A 4-foot-10-inch teen with a juvenile rap sheet filled with petty crimes, a chronic truant with an uneven school record.

And a mother with a raging addiction to heroin.

Devon and a friend had stolen the .22-caliber shotgun from a neighbor's home. Choosing an alley off Belair Road as an improvised target range, the two of them took turns shooting.

At first the gunplay was limited to picking off a few empty 40-ounce malt liquor bottles and rooftop birds.

But then, for reasons that will never be fully known, the danger-ous gunplay turned deadly.

Just as Ms. Letmate was passing the alley along Belair Road, roughly 160 feet away, Devon's brother said the fateful words.

"I bet you can't shoot that lady."

Devon turned around, lifted the gun to his waist, and without even aiming fired off a miracle shot.

The bullet traveled with a marksman's precision. A one-in-a-million volley that the best police sharpshooter couldn't replicate. Traveling 160 feet across Belair Road, the bullet threaded through rush-hour traffic and hit Ms. Letmate squarely in the back of the head.

Devon was standing so far away that a friend of Letmate's who had just greeted her, told us she thought she'd had a stroke.

"She just smiled and then fell down, we didn't know what happened to her," the witness said.

And so on the hot September afternoon when my squad was summoned to a smog-infused street corner of Northeast Baltimore, we literally didn't know if we had a homicide on our hands or an accidental death.

Since most of the witnesses had simply watched Ms. Letmate drop to the ground and die, there wasn't much to start an investigation.

There was a wound at the back of her head, but what could have caused it? A gunshot, a sniper? Who knows?

A few hours later the medical examiner settled the question of how she died. Her wound was the result of a perfectly located gunshot to the back of the head that shattered her skull and scrambled her brains. It was murder.

How though? Where did the bullet come from?

We returned to the crime scene and canvassed the neighborhood, knocking on doors. After a few hours, we got our first break: a witness who happened to be walking down the sidewalk when Ms. Letmate died.

She told us she heard two popping sounds followed by another single pop seconds before Ms. Letmate fell. The witness turned in the direction of the sounds, which she said appeared to be coming from across the street.

The witness saw a black female juvenile and two black male juveniles exit the alley not far from where the popping sounds appeared to have originated. The female was yelling at someone sitting on a nearby porch, trying to convince the bystander the popping sounds were firecrackers set off in the alley.

Then we got a call from a district police officer who introduced us to another witness, a father who overheard his daughter talking to a friend about the shooting. The friend told his daughter that a boy named Devon was playing with a gun when it went off and accidentally shot Ms. Letmate.

Later we returned to the neighborhood to find the daughter's friend. We searched an apartment complex not far from where the shooting occurred, and then knocked on doors along the Belair Road corridor.

Nothing.

But the father had given us another tip. The witness's mother worked at Radio Shack in a suburb called White Marsh.

So we decided to pay her a visit, an encounter that began the process of revealing what this case was all about. It was the girl's mother who revealed to me how the small permutations of how we live, the details unnoticed, often play out in unseen ways.

You could tell she was a hard-working, no-nonsense woman. The minute we told her why we wanted to talk to her daughter, she not only agreed to cooperate, but left work early to find her.

Several hours later both mother and daughter arrived at the Homicide offices.

Before we started the interview, her mother took me aside.

"She's real scared of you," she said. "So I was wondering if you could help me."

I agreed.

"Tell her she has to go to school; she's not going and I don't know what to do," I recall her mother telling me, adding that had her daughter been in school that day, she might not have been hanging around with the boys who we then believed shot Ms. Letmate.

"Okay, but I need you to do me a favor," I said. "If she won't tell me the truth, and I ask you to leave the room, leave," I said.

"Then, I'm going to be rough on her," I said.

"Go right ahead."

Sure enough, when I first started questioning the witness she was tight-lipped. She lied to me with the false bravado of a teenage girl who didn't know any better.

So I turned to her mother.

"You need to leave," I said.

Her daughter panicked.

"I don't want her to leave," she cried.

"Your mother's not going to save you now," I said.

Once her mother was out of the room I let the girl have it. I figured I could do her mother a favor while figuring out what we already knew, so I turned up the heat.

"You better tell me what happened or I'm going to book you and take you over to Central Booking right now and you can sit there for the next 20 years," I threatened.

It didn't take long for her to break.

She gave me all the details of what happened, about the gun, the target practice, the shot that hit and killed Ms. Letmate.

"We saw her fall down, we all ran," she said, subdued and a bit more somber than the defiant teenager I first encountered.

She told us the shooter was Devon, picking him out of a photo array.

Before she left, I made good on my promise to her mother.

"And one other thing," I said. "Starting now, you're going to call me every day when you get to school or I'll come and pick you up myself."

For the next two weeks she called me every morning.

Next we brought in Devon's friend, a teen I'll call "Sam." Sam had been present when Devon made the miracle shot. He recounted the fateful words spoken by Devon's 16-year-old brother.

"He said, 'I bet you can't shoot that lady,'" he recalled. "He told him to shoot her in the leg."

So they just wanted to maim her?

After Sam picked Devon out of a photo array, we had all we needed for a warrant.

We served the arrest warrant later that evening at Devon's Northeast Baltimore home.

On the couch in the living room we found Devon's mother bathed in sweat. She could hardly utter a coherent sentence. She was dopesick and strung out.

It was a bad break, we needed a guardian to allow us to speak with Devon.

Fortunately Devon had a grandmother. A sweet old lady with tired eyes who said she would accompany Devon to Homicide.

And then there was Devon.

Picture a child who stands all of 4-feet-10-inches, a boy who weighs little more than 90 pounds. A small kid with a clear face but dead eyes.

Sitting in the box, he could barely lift his head over the table. How do you write that to make sense?

Blame his heroin-addicted mother for what, being addicted?

Blame his quiet but steady grandmother sitting in the box watching, her eyes swollen with tears?

Devon, despite his size, was not a pushover. That's not to say he was a tough liar, but he seemed to be almost psychologically unaware of what was happening. The idea of murder, of being accused of murder, was beyond his grasp.

As the night wore on, Devon stayed detached. No matter how many times and how many different ways I asked, he always seemed to be casually evasive or simply incapable of admitting he did it.

So I had to wait him out. A coerced confession through intimidation wouldn't sit well with a jury who would see this tiny boy sitting in the defendant's seat — and me, the big bad detective who cursed him out.

So after a half-hour of questioning I brought him back to his cell. Then I sat and waited. Just as he started to fall asleep, I woke him up and brought him back into the box and asked him again.

"Did you shoot the old lady?"

This went on for several hours. In fact, the kid held out longer than I expected.

Finally after five hours of waiting, he admitted it. His head was practically on the floor.

"I shot her," he said.

Then he asked the question that has stuck with me to this day, the unreal question that raises the bigger question.

"Can I go home now?" he asked.

I've looked into the eyes of enough killers to know when someone is lying, even if they're lying well enough to fool themselves.

But this boy had no idea whatsoever of the implications of what he had done. He was clueless.

"No son, you don't understand. You can't go anywhere; you just admitted to murder."

The boy dropped his head to the table as his grandmother burst into tears.

"Ma'am," is all I could manage to say to her.

With that, she gathered Devon into her arms and held him tightly. The boy who murdered another grandmother, probably his own grandmother's age, hugged her back.

She got up to leave, walking out the door of the box, sobbing. Devon looked up to watch her leave. For a second his eyes flickered, as if for a brief moment he understood what was happening.

"Good-bye Grandma."

We booked him on first-degree murder. He pled guilty and is now in jail.

More than likely he'll be out by the time he's 21, that's just three years from now.

By then I hope we will know whose fault it is that Janice Letmate is dead. By then we better know, because we're going to have to teach Devon why the responsibility for her death lies with him.

CASE FILE 4

NICOLE SESKER

What takes hold in a community, if what we think of as a community no longer exists?

That is the question the people who run Baltimore don't want to answer. They don't want to deal with death and despair in the neighborhoods that have been left behind in the 30-year push to develop the Inner Harbor and downtown. They just want to send the police in to clean up, and hopefully cover up the mess.

But if they spent any serious time in the communities they for all intents and purposes ignore, they might learn much about the people whose lives only interest them when mayhem threatens downtown property values — or their reelection prospects.

If you walk down the 3500 block of West Garrison Avenue on any given day, you'll see two distinct types of people: menacing young men in white T-shirts drifting up and down the streets, and old ladies sitting on the porches of worn-down row homes.

Both, in a sense represent the contradictory forces that enable the most desolate parts of this city to survive while remaining for the most part dysfunctional.

The old women are a vestige of the city's past, the sinew, strength and bedrock of what remains of the generations of African-American families that came to Baltimore to work in the Sparrows Point steel mill and Dundalk-area auto factories.

Spend some time in District Court on any given day and you will see old black women sitting on the benches, watching their grandsons and great-grandsons being ferried in and out of courtrooms in shackles.

And on Garrison Avenue in Northwest Baltimore you will see them sitting on their porches, sitting and watching the young men, in many cases their grandsons and great-grandsons, hustling, selling drugs, doing whatever it takes to survive.

It's an unsettling symbiosis. The women in a sense are trapped, too old to move and too poor to get out. They're left to deal with the dead-end lives of their offspring consumed by addiction, poor education, and a criminal justice system that has arrested hundreds of thousands of them with little effect and thought toward a productive outcome.

The older women are the only lifeline to a semblance of order for many of these young men whose lives are short, filled with violence, and in their own minds, I'm sure, hopeless.

It's just the leftovers of a healthy community really, a worn-out fabric that may be irreparably frayed beyond repair.

I mention this world which few people understand because this very block, 3500 West Garrison Avenue in Park Heights, became the final resting place of Nicole Sesker, the stepdaughter of my mentor, former Police Commissioner Leonard Hamm. And when I say few people understand it, I mean it's really not what you think.

In fact, the misapprehension of how these neighborhoods came to be, and by extension how Nicole Sesker came to die there, is one is the biggest problems this city faces.

For beyond racism, beyond political corruption and police brutality is the psychological and social isolation we've created in these communities which the powers-that-be deem suitable only for cops, crooks, and as I said before, impoverished old ladies.

We keep making the same mistakes, because we don't understand. We don't understand why the women remain, why they won't abandon a lost generation and mere memories of a better past.

All communities, dysfunctional or not, have a way of becoming self-sustaining. In neighborhoods like West Garrison in Northwest Baltimore the relationships I described have evolved as the tide of economic opportunity receded. The petty hustle, the small-time dealing, the occasional prostitution sustains them, keeps the electricity on in a row home on the verge of collapse, food on the table, a pack of cigarettes in the basement.

And at the core of this communal despair are the old women, the women who have watched the city fall apart, watched their families ravaged by poverty, drugs, and the lure of crime. And yet they ultimately refuse to let go.

Garrison Avenue in Northwest Baltimore is a death trap of sorts for the younger women. With drug dealers setting up shop in abandoned row homes on Belvedere Avenue, women with drug habits they can't support tend to congregate in the area, eking out a living by turning $20 tricks and sleeping wherever and with whomever will offer shelter.

I was on the tail end of an overnight shift when the call came from a neighbor who spotted the body of a woman under a porch in a nearby row home while taking out the trash in June of 2008. Shortly, I was in the back of an alley behind West Garrison Avenue staring at the body of my mentor's stepdaughter, although at that time I didn't know who she was.

When we arrive at any probable homicide scene, the first thing we do is try to identify the body. Knowing the victim's identity, as you can imagine, is a critical detail for any investigation. The body was lying in a nest of scattered trash, empty Instant Lipton Soup containers, discarded Newport cigarette packs, bottle caps and cigarette butts.

She was a fairly young, African-American woman. Her skirt was pulled down to her ankles, and her panties slid down her legs. She had a blue bandanna around her head.

We canvassed the scene, but could not identify her.

In the alley behind Garrison Avenue, a small crowd had gathered a few houses down the street. I noticed a woman who looked particularly distraught. I asked her to come with me.

"Do you know who that is?" I asked her as she trembled.

She let out a quick scream. "Oh my God! that's the commissioner's daughter," she said. "That's Nicole."

"That's Nicole Sesker," she repeated.

"Are you sure?" I asked.

"Yes," she said, breaking down into tears.

For a moment I was dumbfounded, in shock. I knew right away which commissioner she meant.

Commissioner Leonard Hamm, one of my mentors, a cop I respected, who trained me at the Police Academy. Now I was staring at the body of his daughter, half clothed, discarded under a porch like a used rag.

I realized this was a big case, so I immediately expanded the crime scene, and I mean expanded for several blocks.

"Everyone back," I shouted, ordering the patrol officers on the scene to cordon off the area for several blocks.

The crowd that had assembled not far from Nicole's body was soon gone.

Then I got a call from Police Commissioner Frederick Bealefeld.

"What do you have?" he asked.

"Hamm's daughter," I said.

"Keep me informed," he replied.

Now if you're wondering how the stepdaughter of a police commissioner ends up dead under a porch in an area known for prostitution and drug dealing, just remember what I said. Think of Northwest as a metaphor for the entire city. The beautiful Inner Harbor surrounded by million-dollar condominiums less than a quarter-mile away from the crime-ridden neighborhood called Pigtown and the trendy Fells Point historic waterfront adjacent to the Perkins Homes Housing Project.

Less than half a mile from where Nicole died is the Pimlico Race Course, where the second jewel of horse racing's Triple Crown, the Preakness Stakes, is broadcast 'round the world.

Great wealth and great poverty side by side, like a third-world country, the gulf in between becomes a vacuum that sucks us all in, eventually.

But back to the crime scene.

After canvassing the weed-filled backyard for clues, and supervising the removal of the body by the State Medical Examiner's office, I had to perform one of the most awkward and unpleasant tasks of my career.

As I've said before, one of the worst parts of my job is dealing with the living, the people left behind. But never in my career did I think I would have to tell a former commissioner that his daughter had been murdered.

Nicole's life, her struggle with drugs and prostitution, was no secret. In fact, she ended up on Page 1 of the New York Times, after a reporter discovered her on the streets of Northwest Baltimore while her father sat in the commissioner's chair.

It was a national story, the veteran police commissioner in a city wracked by violence, with his outspoken stepdaughter talking about a life of prostitution and drug dealing, sleeping under the porch of an abandoned home for nearly a decade.

When we arrived at former Commissioner Hamm's house, we saw Commissioner Frederick Bealefeld leaving. He didn't say much, though I'm sure it wasn't a happy moment for him to have to inform his predecessor that his daughter was murdered on his watch.

Inside, Hamm sat us down at a living room table. He was, and still is, a stoic man who doesn't show much emotion. A big bear of a man really who rarely smiles or lets you know what he's thinking.

"I just want you to know sir, that we are doing everything we can to solve this case. I'll be handling it personally," I told him.

"I know," he said, shaking his head.

And then he said something that to this day I still can't believe.

"You know," he said, staring off into space, "Nicole told me that bastard picked her up one night."

"Excuse me sir," I said.

"The bastard picked up my daughter," he continued, mentioning the name of a former Baltimore City police commander. "That bastard picked her up one night, when she was on the street."

We didn't say much after that and neither did he. I don't know why he decided to drop that bomb on the day of his daughter's murder, but it certainly wasn't anything I expected to hear. I don't think even "The Wire" could top that.

But of course, when we left Hamm's home, I didn't have the luxury of time to contemplate the sexual escapades of a former top cop. Instead, I had to solve a murder.

At least that's what I thought.

The medical examiner ruled that Nicole was strangled. Whoever did it, killed her with his hands, then dragged her body under the only empty row home on the block, our first clue that the perpetrator probably lived nearby.

There was unknown DNA under her fingernails.

But the case that I promised Leonard Hamm I would manage personally became embroiled in the politics of Homicide, the same style of politics that I believe has a lot to do with the desolation and neglect of huge swathes of the impoverished city.

Major Frederick Tabor, who headed the Homicide Division at the time, ordered an analysis of recent murders of women in the city along with their records. Most of our homicide victims are men, and most are shot. So when a woman is strangled, it's always good to check for similar cases to find a common pattern, or suspect.

What we found was disturbing, and made the already intense publicity surrounding Nicole's murder even worse.

Since April of that year, four other women with records of prostitution had been strangled. Each one worked on the street like Nicole, each one had drug issues and was transient.

The death of Nicole focused media attention on sex workers, and it wasn't long before stories began to appear revealing the fact that a total of five prostitutes including Nicole had recently been strangled to death.

As pressure from the media grew, one would think Homicide

would get its act together and start working the streets to solve the cases, including Nicole's.

But not in Baltimore.

As the media began speculating about the possibility of a connection between the five cases — and worse yet, a serial killer — the city's public affairs officer told the press that the commissioner was forming a task force.

Of course, there were no plans for a task force when the announcement was made, and in reality the last thing anyone in the Baltimore Police Department wanted to find was a serial killer.

So when it came time to convene this task force to investigate the death of Nicole Sesker and the four other women — Elizabeth Garrett, Amanda Bishop, Yolanda Brown, and Brenda Hatfield — the entire enterprise came down to one thing: who gets the overtime.

I knew the moment they put the team together there was little interest in solving any of the cases except Sesker's. Several of the detectives were the laziest on the floor, but one thing the task force all but guaranteed was lots of overtime and very little work.

Meanwhile, I was taken off the Sesker case despite my promise to Hamm. Even though my squad had the second-highest clearance rate on the floor, I was told I had enough cases to work on. So in the end, the politics of pay, not who could really solve the cases, dictated who was assigned to what.

And to this day, not one of the cases of the four other women who were strangled has been solved.

To me, being taken off the case was truly a setback, because I already had a suspect.

As I said before, in that neighborhood you have two things, old ladies on porches, and their assorted progeny with a variety of problems.

And from my initial interview with the man who lived next door to where Nicole was found, it was pretty clear the suspect lived on the block, or at least someone who lived there knew who did it.

Within a day of canvassing the area I had a suspect, a man with the nickname "Peanut." His cousin lived next door at 3511 West Garrison, along with his mother.

Just from my initial conversation I could tell that Peanut's cousin was lying.

After he let it slip that Peanut was with Nicole just before she died, I thought I had good case.

But then the case was taken away. Another detective took over and had problems with the case because Peanut's mother, one of the old ladies on the porch, lied for him. My replacement was never able to get a confession.

Still, DNA evidence tied Peanut, a man named Joseph Antonio Bonds, to Nicole. The young detective who took the case could have used help; I think I could have worked with Bonds' family and gotten him to talk.

But instead, they relied on DNA, and after they arrested Bonds, the case fell apart in court.

A witness who saw Sesker alive after Bonds allegedly choked her, and an inconclusive medical examiner's report that said Bonds could not have killed her, led to what is known as an "Alford plea," where the defendant admits that there is enough evidence to convict him but is then allowed to assert his innocence while pleading guilty in exchange for a lighter sentence.

Bonds received a sentence of 20 years with all but eight suspended. With good behavior, he could be out in four. Just four years for taking the life of a police commissioner's daughter.

Not that I think there should be different tiers of justice. But in the end, we couldn't even successfully prosecute a case that supposedly had the full force of the department behind it. In fact, given the doubts that were raised during the trial I wonder if we even had the right man.

And then there are the four other women whose cases remain open. Their murders will probably go unsolved, even though an entire squad of so-called task force detectives made tens of thousands of dollars in overtime pay for making coffee and watching baseball on television, on the job.

In the meantime, nothing has changed in Northwest Baltimore. The old women sit on their porches, looking out for their kinfolk.

And with a department like ours that can't even protect its own, who can blame them?

CASE FILE 5

NICOLE EDMONDS

Nicole Edmonds

Let me ask you a question. If you had just finished stabbing someone to death, would you pick up their unfinished sandwich and start eating it?

Sounds like the behavior of a serial killer or stone cold sociopath, right?

But that's exactly what 16-year-old Lataye King did right after she stabbed 17-year-old Nicole Edmonds twice in the chest.

She and Kendrick McCain, just 15, had chased Nicole and her half-brother Marcus from the North Avenue Light Rail Station. Their motive: they wanted Nicole's cellphone.

Both siblings ran for their lives, still dressed in the Wendy's uniforms they wore at the Linthicum restaurant where they worked. Marcus, being a boy and a good bit faster, got away.

But Lataye, along with Kendrick, caught up with Nicole just under the North Avenue Bridge. There, off a dirt path sided by burnt patches of grass, Kendrick slapped Nicole across the face, and then Lataye stabbed her to death.

As Nicole lay bleeding on the ground, Lataye picked up Nicole's cellphone, and perhaps as an afterthought, snatched up the Wendy's bag Nicole had taken from work with a chicken filet sandwich inside.

Then, just moments later, Lataye walked across the North Avenue Bridge eating the meal taken from Nicole's dying hands.

I think about this case quite a bit.

I think about it because of all the extremes it represents in this city, and how it is an example for me of why Baltimore may never fully right itself.

Not simply because of corruption or police apathy or poverty or the variety of other reasons I've discussed in this narrative, but as a result of the long-lasting effects of the violence that radiates in waves throughout the community and leaves wounds so deep I believe they will remain forever unhealed.

A murder may take only a few minutes of bad judgment and horrific behavior, but the effects of violently removing someone from this earth changes so many lives for the worse, that after awhile there may be no way to heal.

There have been more than 5,000 murders in this city since I first put on my BPD uniform. It's the number at root of the exponential spirals of loss that radiate from the taking of life, the existential wounds that have created the void that is at the very core of this city. A void that grows deeper and darker with each murder.

Nicole and her brother came from a good family. Her father is a pastor.

She had a bright future. She was a good student. She worked hard. She was home schooled, preparing for college.

And she was killed for a cellphone. A cellphone!

What on earth drives a person to kill for a cellphone? And what does it say about the soul of Baltimore if all it takes to pick up a deadly weapon and drive it into the chest of a promising young woman is the desire to have a cellphone?

The path that turned Lataye King into a killer was forged years before she picked up a knife and plunged it into Nicole's chest. But more on that later.

I will never forget that night at University of Maryland Shock Trauma after Nicole was murdered.

When murder victims die in the emergency room, their bodies are taken to a special section of the floor, placed behind a curtain where they are wrapped in a blanket and prepared for transport to the medical examiner's office for autopsy.

When I arrived, I didn't know that Nicole's father, Wayne Edmonds, was already there.

He is a tall, hulking man, a pastor at the Tabernacle Church of Deliverance in East Baltimore. So when I stepped behind the curtain, what I saw was as painful and disturbing as any crime scene.

Pastor Edmonds was bent over his daughter's body, his broad shoulders slumped at his sides leaning against the wall. He was crying. A grown bear of a man reduced to tears, scarred for life because of a teenager's stupid decision and violent action.

As I've said, one of the worst parts about being a homicide detective is dealing with the living, the relatives, the people left behind.

What do you say to a man who just lost his daughter in an instant, whose beautiful baby girl was reduced to a corpse over a cellphone? I think all the murderers and corrupt politicians sitting in Central Booking should be forced to be the first person to tell a mother or father their child is dead.

What do you say to a man who has just lost his daughter?

All I try to do is be straightforward and sincere. And in cases like this, I go a bit further.

When I saw Pastor Edmonds crying over his daughter's dead body, when I saw the pain in his eyes, the complete and utter agony of loss, I didn't tell him I was sorry for his loss, or that I understood, or even try to console him.

In that moment, I had only one thing to say and it came out of my mouth as naturally as the air I breathe.

"I promise you I will find the person who killed your daughter."

That was all I said. He looked at me, and I could tell it was all that he wanted to hear.

When I stepped out of that room I told myself, no matter what, I was keeping my word. We would find whoever did this and we would find them now.

So when I returned to the Homicide floor later that evening I did so with my promise to him and myself in mind.

The first thing we did was put out Marcus's descriptions of Nicole's killers to all the district patrol and detective units, a move that would pay off later.

Which brings me back to my point about murder, about how it radiates through a community, shattering the coherence of people's lives forever. Nicole's brother Marcus was just such a casualty, collateral damage, so to speak.

When I first spoke with him at the hospital he was inconsolable. From his point of view, he had failed his sister; he now blamed himself for her death.

In his eyes I could see the agony of self doubt and despair, the type of despondency that overwhelms those close to the victim, particularly in cases where the relatives truly believe they could have prevented the murder.

I remember putting my hand on his shoulder. I knew I had to say something. If the boy, only 17, continued to blame himself for his sister's death his father might lose another child.

"There's only one person to blame for your sister's death and it's not you," I told him.

Truthfully I don't know if he heard me. He was too overwhelmed with grief.

But I do know this much: The pain he was feeling, the permanent wound opened by watching his sister die and feeling responsible for her death would never be healed. Who knows how it will impact his life? Who knows how his life could have been different had a couple of teens not decided to commit murder over a cellphone?

We began reviewing the tapes from Light Rail trains running on the evening the murder occurred.

At first we found nothing, as Maryland Transit Authority police were unable to locate the tapes from the train that Nicole and Marcus were riding.

The next day after we returned to the scene to canvass it again, I received a call that they had found the tapes.

When we picked up the tapes we were initially hopeful, as Nicole and Marcus could be clearly seen exiting the train. We could also see what seemed like another set of teens exiting at a different door.

But unfortunately even after we turned the tapes over to a special unit to be enhanced, the images were of such poor quality that we couldn't use them to identify the suspects. Still, we took the tapes to the Hartford County Sheriff's department for further work.

In the meantime we caught a break. Southern District Patrol arrested a teen for shoplifting at a Sam's Club. The suspect said he knew who killed Nicole Edmonds.

He told us he had overheard several of his friends talking about the stabbing. One of those friends, he identified as Kendrick McCain.

And then we caught another break. The enhanced video netted several images of possible suspects.

But the minute Kendrick walked onto the Homicide floor I stopped worrying about the video: I knew we were going to solve this case.

Kendrick was scared. He was fidgety in the box, and could hardly look me in the eye. And I knew before I even asked the first question, he was guilty. The only thing I was trying to figure out was when he was going to tell me.

So I laid it out for him.

It was a routine I've used before. I call it "a set of options." A choice between telling me what I already know — now, or later.

"What level of trouble do you want?" I ask. Then I show them, using my hand, waving it front of them to illustrate from low to high just how much trouble they can find by putting off telling me the truth.

"You tell us now," I say, and you can be in this much trouble. But if you don't talk, it will only get worse," I say, raising my hand higher.

Fortunately, Kendrick was listening. He was hardly a thug, just a misdirected punk bereft of any sense of right and wrong.

After my little speech, it didn't take long for him to confess.

"I'm not going down alone," he said, proceeding to tell us he "only" slapped Nicole, and it was a girl named Lataye King who stabbed her.

"Only."

I don't think he understood that "only" slapping Nicole made him just as guilty as the other teen he fingered. It didn't matter though, because that night we charged him with first-degree murder and began looking for King.

It took the Warrant Apprehension Task Force less than a day to find Lataye King, living in the apartment of a guardian in Suitland, in Prince George's County.

And while Kendrick seemed like a misdirected teen — as I said before — Lataye was an entirely different type of suspect.

There are children I come across, teens barely, who have personalities so cold and indifferent it throws me off guard. I'm not talking about a sociopath with an icy exterior and callous persona; I mean children who seem too off and far-gone to reach, simply lost in the world and indifferent to anything that touches them.

Lataye was a good example.

Sitting in the box, she looked unkempt, her hair wild and uncombed. Yet her gaze was so insolent, so dead it was disturbing. Truthfully it's hard to describe what it's like to sit across from someone so young who appears to be devoid of empathy, really just empty.

From the beginning I knew she wasn't going to talk. And sure enough, she didn't.

I told her what we knew already, how we placed her at the scene with the video footage and Kendrick's statement, but she didn't seem to care.

Instead she just sat there, staring into space, a million miles away but not really anywhere at all.

After she refused to give a statement, we obtained a search warrant for the apartment where she was picked up.

There we found several bags full of clothes, a sweatshirt and sweatpants with blood stains. We also found a black leather woman's purse, a purse that Nicole's father later identified as hers.

We tried for several days to locate Lataye's legal guardian, a woman named Tonya Wilson. I don't think we ever located her.

With the physical evidence, the purse, and Kendrick's confession, we charged Lataye with first-degree murder. She pled guilty and received a life sentence with all but 25 years suspended. The judge remanded her to a psychiatric prison.

Yet it was the aftermath of this case that disturbed me most, the study in contrasts that emerged as the lives of both teens were revealed over time.

After the case, city prosecutors did an informal study of teenage murderers like Lataye. Turns out she was a high school dropout with a history of truancy, a runaway. She did not have a family. Her mother had disowned her; her father, unknown. Her psychological profile was so alarming even prosecutors recommended she be institutionalized rather than sent to prison.

Meanwhile, as the media continued to cover the case an entirely different picture emerged of the young woman she killed.

Nicole was a good student with plans to go to college. A young woman with a beautiful voice who used to lead the choir in her father's church. Her parents had pulled her out of Frederick Douglass Senior High in Northwest Baltimore — where Supreme Court Justice Thurgood Marshall once went to school — because they feared for her safety.

And now she lay in the morgue, her prospective future snuffed out. Meanwhile Lataye would spend most of her adult life incarcerated because of what seemed like a moment's indiscretion.

But this incident was in fact something that had been brewing since the day Lataye was born into a world that really didn't want her. And so, one shattered life, Lataye's, led to another, and then another — what some might call a vicious cycle.

But for me, it seems more truthful to call it an inevitable result of a city full of people who are invisible unless they pick up a knife and kill someone. It's only through violence that they speak to us, and only after they have killed someone that we listen.

CASE FILE 6

Mother-Daughter Murder

William Jones

William Jones had finished stabbing 17-year-old Quira Lybal to death.

Quira lay splayed on the cold hardwood floor of her bedroom covered in blood. In fact, he had stabbed her so hard and so many times that the entire room was awash in it.

But Jones was not finished. Quira's mother, 59-year-old Deborah Beard, was still alive.

She was screaming from the bedroom on the other side of their first floor apartment. The elderly diabetic whose legs had recently been amputated was forced to sit on her bed and listen to the death-throe howls of her daughter.

"She wouldn't stop screaming," Jones later told me of Beard's lamentations, shaking his head.

"I messed up," said the 6-foot-7 425-lb. man.

Indeed Jones had messed up. And it would get worse.

But before I tell the rest, you need to know a little more about William Jones. In particular, why he was inside the first floor apartment at 5533 Middleton Court early that morning in December of 2009.

Violence in Baltimore is indiscriminate. It can flare up anywhere at any time, unlike in other cities where to a certain extent violence is segregated.

I'm not talking about the random domestic dispute that ends with the murder of a wife or even a husband, I'm talking about real mayhem, like the case of William Jones.

Jones, like so many other sociopaths in Baltimore took the pathology of violence to a whole new level, as you will soon find out.

He was an alcoholic. That morning he was scheduled to check into rehab in Philadelphia. But sometime earlier the evening before the murders, his wife took the children and left, probably because he decided to spend his last few hours before rehab getting drunk.

Distraught, Jones went downstairs to talk to Quira. She was 17 years old, a little overweight but pretty and by all accounts friendly.

Jones had been having sex with her. Now that his wife had left, he later recounted, he told Quira that he was ready to start a relationship with her.

But the young teen wasn't interested, telling Jones she wanted nothing more than sex, and least of all a relationship with a man nearly twice her age.

And then, Jones told us, he snapped.

Veteran homicide detectives play a game. We try to stump one another with street names. We name an obscure street, and then challenge our opponent to name a case or a few details that prove he or she has been there.

It's a tough game. After a couple of years in the unit you've been to a lot of places; the game can last a half-dozen rounds before someone is stumped. And that's saying a lot because there are over a thousand named streets in Baltimore.

However Middleton Court is a street I will never forget, a one-and-a-half-block-long byway nestled less than a mile from two local Catholic colleges on one side and one of the most violent sections of town on the other.

We arrived at 5533 Middleton after a neighbor called 911 reporting screams from the house. I took a look around the neighborhood as I always do.

It's a ritual to get a feel for the environment, the world in which the crime occurred.

I make a mental note of who's standing around, who's interested in what's going on. It gives me a start on piecing things together. Maybe I see gang colors, maybe I see a witness whose expression tells me he or she wants to talk.

And maybe I bump into the suspect's mother, which is what happened in this case.

But more on that later.

Like a lot of neighborhoods I'd been to, there was no outward sign of the extraordinary violence that occurs behind closed doors. Just well-maintained row home after well-maintained row home, and this neighborhood was no exception.

Let me say that I know it is a common theme of crime books to recount unspeakable acts behind the pristine façade of suburbs. That's not what I'm talking about here.

First, the Baltimore neighborhoods are simple, not a spiffed up suburban style. Second, these neat little communities are sometimes the scenes of the most violent crimes, and not just one, but a series of crimes that turn placid environments into a veritable war zone.

There aren't any rotting ghetto tenement homes and burned out vacant lots that mark the place where safety ends and violence begins. Instead, all you see here is one little pleasant neighborhood after another where residents have a penchant for killing each other.

Take for example the little patch of tidy row homes where the killers of Councilman Ken Harris lived. It's a neat little neighborhood of one well-manicured lawn after another just behind the Northwood Shopping Center, not far from Morgan State University. It was among those little patches of grass that a string of homicides was produced, nearly bringing Baltimore to its knees.

Harris was a respected former city councilman, a success story who emerged from the ghetto to become a well-liked and outspoken community leader.

One September evening in 2008 he was standing outside the New Haven Lounge, a popular jazz club in Northeast Baltimore, talking to the club's owner. Three young men approached brandishing guns, ordering Harris and the owner inside.

Harris ran for his car, and as he got inside one of the robbers shot him in the back, killing him at the scene.

All three of the suspects came from the same neighborhood, the scene of a previous murder and the subsequent slaying of a witness tied to Harris's case. Three execution-style slayings against the backdrop of well-kept row homes and quiet streets.

And this was just how Jones's neighborhood looked. Chinquapin Elementary School stood just across the street; tidy row homes and freshly mowed lawns extended for blocks.

But inside was a murder scene that would make Hannibal Lecter blush.

But back to the crime itself.

Jones was sitting in the bedroom, Quira lay dead on the floor. Her mother was still screaming, so he had to make a decision. Kill the mother? Flee the scene? He didn't give us much insight into what he did next, only that the screaming bothered him.

At some point, he left the bedroom, walked across the living room and picked up her mother.

Then he carried her into Quira's bedroom, placed her on the bed. For a moment, we think, he just sat there. Maybe he wanted to show Quira's mother the body of her daughter before he stabbed her too. Maybe he had a moment of regret or compassion. We don't really know what he was thinking because he told us he blacked out.

The one thing I do know is that the last thing that woman saw on this earth was the bludgeoned body of her daughter lying on the floor in a pool of blood.

So then, probably without pretense or ceremony, Jones lifted a knife over his head and proceeded to stab Deborah Beard over 20 times.

After he finished, Jones inexplicably decided to move Quira's body. At first he couldn't get her to budge.

"Dead weight is heavy," he told us casually during our interview.

So Jones took off his belt and looped it around Quira's neck, dragging her body into the living room.

Next, we believe, he took off his clothes, perhaps with the hope of disposing of them.

But while he stood naked in the middle of the apartment, his mother arrived.

As I said before we actually bumped into her walking into the apartment later on. She at first lied to us and said she was simply responding to a call from a neighbor. But we soon discovered she had already been to the scene, and had driven her son to her house and instructed him to take a shower.

"What have you done?" she later told us she said when she arrived.

"I killed them, Mom," he said. "Take me to Canada."

"I watch enough 'CSI,' I can take care of this," she later told us she said to her son.

So without much thought about the young teen and her mother, who was not yet dead, Jones's mother drove him home and told him to take a shower. She then returned to the scene, which is where we encountered her.

If you had seen the crime scene, this type of calculated thinking would unnerve you even more than the blood-spattered walls and the legless woman gasping for breath on the bedroom floor not far from her daughter's now bloated corpse.

This is the reason I remain wary of this town. Baltimore has been painted in so many different ways, but none of them is real.

Because it takes a certain type of person to remain calm in the face of that sort of bloodshed, a cold interior that allows you to devise a way to cover up a crime that is so horrific.

However it's not that we all don't have the instinct to evade responsibility for our misdeeds. Nobody wants to go to jail.

But to walk into that type of carnage, to immediately spring into action, to corral your son and try to construct an alibi and cover up evidence of that magnitude speaks to a different way of thinking.

It gives me pause every time I arrive on the scene in a neighborhood like Jones's. I look around and see the well-kept homes, the children and the dogs, the seemingly unremarkable un-urban city.

But behind those front doors lies a cruelty that seems to be boundless, too. An even-tempered practice of killing that pervades almost every neighborhood in the city.

Just before I entered the crime scene, I received a call from a family friend. She had heard something about a homicide involving a friend. It took me a minute but I soon realized she was taking about Ms. Beard and her daughter. "My cousin was distraught," she said, referring to the person who had told her about the murders. "Both the mother and daughter were sweet, churchgoing people."

What a waste, I thought. What a horrible fate for two innocents.

Later, when we had Jones sitting in the box, he hardly seemed aware of what he'd done.

The man who looked like he could walk into an NFL game and take his rightful place at left tackle seemed more like a drunk battling a hangover than someone who had committed brutal premeditated murder.

He told us that he blacked out that evening, and the next thing he knew he was sitting on his mother's porch.

Then he asked a question.

"How's Quira?"

"She didn't make it," I answered.

And that's when he buried his face in his hands and admitted that he had "messed up."

But that didn't mean he had murdered her, or even committed a crime, from his perspective.

For a while we went around in circles, Jones still sticking to his story that he didn't remember anything.

So I played the one card that I have found can still reach the heart of even the most hardened killer.

"This case is going to trial, and your mother is going to have to testify."

It was the first thing I said the entire evening that seemed to get his attention.

"My mother? Why does she have to testify?"

"Because she's a witness, so you better be prepared, and she may be charged, too," I said.

And with that he broke.

"Okay, "he said evenly. "I did it."

Funny how the bond between a mother and son can still be strong in a man who took a child away from a mother while she lay in the next room screaming. Strange that he could have carried the bereaved woman to a bed and murdered her in cold blood while her daughter lay dead on the floor.

It makes you wonder about this town. It makes you think twice before you get out of your car.

It makes you wonder what's really going on.

CASE FILE 7

Baby Murdered

I was sitting in my kitchen when I saw the bag.

It was a black Nike pull-string bag like the one my daughter uses to carry her schoolbooks.

I was talking to my wife when my daughter walked in, the bag slung over her shoulder.

It stopped me in mid-sentence. I was getting pulled back.

Any homicide detective knows what that means. Something triggers an association, an object, a gesture, even an odor. And suddenly your mind travels 60 miles south, to a point three days earlier.

Next thing I know I am standing in the woods in Druid Hill Park. It is dark; I can barely see my own feet.

I had just walked up a hill near a clearing in the woods. The ground was hardened by a December cold snap and iced over with a trace of snow.

We had been following a man named "Solemana Smith."

He had shown up in Homicide a few hours earlier. He was distraught and jittery.

I sat him down in the box.

"She showed me," he mumbled before I could ask a question.

"Showed you what?" I asked.

"Where she put him."

"Who?"

"My son. She showed me where she buried him."

As he sat at the table trembling, I had to make a quick calculation.

I knew what he was telling me. I knew where this was going before we got there. But I also had to get some sense if he was a suspect or a witness. I had to know if he was reporting a crime, or concealing one.

So I asked him a few questions, loaded questions that might give me a sense of his role in what sounded like an extremely unpleasant situation.

"So you put the baby in the hole?" I said, asking him to repeat what he just told me to gauge just how involved he was.

When he answered the question in the negative without acknowledging my lead, I decided for the moment he was probably telling the truth.

So there we were, standing on the hill in the middle of Druid Hill Park staring at a hole covered with trash. Detective Juan Diaz's curiosity had gotten the better of him when we arrived in the park. He started leading the way.

I called him back and took him aside.

"Do you know where he's going?" I asked Diaz.

"No," he answered.

"Then let him show us," I said, pointing at Smith.

The hole was covered by an upside down two-liter Pepsi bottle, a tennis shoe, and some candy wrappers.

Without a shred of moonlight, we carefully removed the bottle.

Then I saw the bag, the black Nike bag stuffed inside the hole. I could see the outline of what looked like a small animal, the tracings of a rotted arm.

But it was too dark to go further. We called the Crime Lab.

Thirty minutes later, with floodlights bearing down on the small two-foot gap in the ground, a Crime Lab technician untied the bag and pulled the strings so that a small gap revealed what was inside.

It was the tiny almost too small shoulder of a baby. A baby buried in a black Nike bag.

Homicide detectives compartmentalize. That's no secret. It's something everybody does, from the nurses that care for the dying to firefighters who remove burnt bodies from fire-torn buildings. You have to if you want to remain sane, to keep the somewhat small sense of comfort, illusory or not, that people don't die violently every day.

Sometimes it works and sometimes it doesn't, like in the case of the black Nike bag.

And what the bag brings back is what you can't shut out, what seeps through the cracks into your life outside the streets.

Human nature.

Why do people behave so differently 20 miles north of Baltimore City? Why don't people in Hunt Valley or Monkton shove babies into bags? Are people really that different in essence? Or are we essentially the same, just shaped by our environment or by the neighborhood we live in?

This is not a complicated question, but it has some important implications.

People kill regularly in Baltimore. Twenty miles north they don't — at least not regularly. What should I conclude from that? What type of boundaries of the land have we created that also take hold of the mind?

Mind you, people kill everywhere. We live in a relatively murderous country.

But Baltimore is the apex of that violent strain. And thus the city begs the question: Are these people naturally amoral or prone to violence? Or, and this is a thought that bothers me more, is the violence I see here simply a payback for the years of neglect and cruelty we inflict upon the less fortunate?

Better put, are we civilized or can we ill afford to be civil?

Standing on that hill watching the crime technician carefully place the baby into a body bag to transport it back to the medical examiner's office, I wondered if I could answer that question soon enough to keep the next baby alive.

But that would have to wait. We needed to solve this case.

After we found the baby, we took Smith back to Homicide. Still obviously shaken, he gave us a taped statement.

He told us the baby's name, Rajasthan Haynie. He was born just 44 days before his mother, Lakesha Haynie, stuffed him in the ground, Smith told us.

The father said Lakesha had taken him to the makeshift grave, removed the soda bottle grave marker, and pulled out the body to show him. He said she told him the baby had died by suffocating in bed when she had accidentally placed her hand over the baby's mouth, and she had decided to bury him in the park, close to her apartment.

The father had given us enough to get a warrant. Now all we had to do was find the woman who killed her own child.

Once I gave the Warrant Apprehension Task Force her last known address, I called Social Services.

I learned that Lakesha was not supposed to have children. Maryland State Child Protective Services had already warned her that if she gave birth again the child would immediately be taken away. We were told she was mentally ill. Maybe schizophrenic, maybe bipolar.

Even worse, her four other children were in protective custody living with foster parents. This woman had no business bringing another child into the world. Sadly however, although she was unfit to be a mother, she was clever enough to skirt the law.

The best we could figure, Lakesha, had given birth outside of a hospital. Then, because she knew the baby would be taken away, she traveled to Philadelphia to get medical treatment for the child when he became ill.

Hospital officials in Philadelphia sent us records of Lakesha and her son's hospital stay.

So when she arrived at Homicide we were prepared — and so was she.

I guess, looking back on my first encounter with her, she had to a certain extent erased the baby from her mind.

She entered the box calm and collected. Not necessarily the type of confidence of a sane killer, but more like the serenity of a person too nuts to realize she had killed a baby.

Her hair shot into the air like someone who had been electrocuted. Her eyes were dead straight, almost hard-wired into an unnatural neutral.

For the first 20 minutes as we asked her about Rajasthan, she played dumb.

"I have four children and they're not with me," she said matter of factly.

"Just four?" I asked, wanting to give her an opportunity to back herself into a corner.

"Just four," she said.

"What about this child," I asked casually, showing her the hospital's report. "What about Rajasthan?"

She didn't say anything at first. I think for a moment she couldn't process the fact that the baby who had disappeared in her mind had suddenly taken form on a piece of paper she never expected us to find.

Bear in mind, that when we raided Lakesha's apartment, there was not a single trace of evidence anybody lived there, let alone a child. She had scrubbed the floors, thrown out the bed sheets, and scoured the walls.

Like I said before, she was crazy to a point.

But at that moment I could see wheels turning in her head.

"I didn't kill him," she said abruptly. "He suffocated in bed," she added, barely acknowledging the child she had brought into the world and then violently removed in little more than a month.

"Then I buried him."

It was an interesting theory, but the ME initially disagreed: The child died from blunt force trauma.

We told her as much, but she refused to budge. "He suffocated," she insisted.

"Listen," I said. "His skull was fractured, that's what caused his death."

"I watch CSI, you can't prove that," she replied.

So now she was both crazy but sane enough to invoke the "CSI effect" prosecutors are always talking about. She was insistent that we couldn't prove that her baby was killed by her hand because of something she had seen on television.

It was like a gambit on a game show. Like the issue wasn't the violent death of a 44-day-old child, or the violent act she committed, but simply a matter of using an explanation based on the misapprehension of a television show.

And then she told me something that has stuck with me ever since. I'm not sure why she said it, maybe she thought it would explain the head wound.

She described to us how the child wouldn't fit into the hole she had dug. How she had grabbed onto a tree and stomped her foot down on top of the baby's head.

She told it to me as if she had was describing how she had changed a tire. There she was, a mother, sane enough to cover up her crime, but at the same time methodically cruel enough to stomp on her child's head like it was a loose root.

Still, even after telling us how she stuffed him into the hole, she would not admit she murdered the baby. She was both stubborn and stupid, refusing to acknowledge what was already evident.

But it didn't matter if she talked. We had the father's statement, which was enough to indict her on first-degree murder charges. Our best theory is that one day, enraged, she hit the child so hard she cracked his skull and killed him.

But truthfully we may never know.

And so I'm left holding the bag, so to speak, the Nike bag, the image that tears down the boundaries of the world where women kill their babies — and the world where they don't.

The problem is, I'm not totally convinced the two worlds are so completely distinct.

A world where a woman could simply stuff her own flesh and blood down a hole and then tacitly admit what she had done without a trace of emotion, is not as difficult for me to understand as it once was.

In a way I'm completely familiar with it.

Her behavior, while reprehensible, isn't too far away from the psyche of a detached homicide detective. It's not that much of a departure from some of the detectives who laugh over a body. Or don't show up to work for weeks at a time while telling a family they're making progress.

Was her cruelty that different?

Whatever the case, I remember the next day searching the park for evidence, when one of my detectives called me over to a tree. There, high up the branches was a baby jump seat and a few blankets. I remember the blankets were blue.

We needed to call firefighters to retrieve the leftover items from the child's brief life. A blanket that might have covered him on his first day of life, and now, somehow Lakesha had managed to throw it along with the jump seat 20 feet into the air.

She must have used every bit of strength within her compact, heavyset frame to do it.

As I stood watching a firefighter dislodge the dead baby's jump seat from a branch, I thought about how much effort a human being will put into covering up a murder, and how little they will do to prevent it.

It's sort of like the same rollercoaster we ride in this city. We wait for bad things to happen, and then we react. We hope that we can somehow distance ourselves from the parts of human nature that make it possible to kill and then forget.

We hope in the end, that we're exceptions to the rule, in both our behavior and our mortality. That is what keeps us sane, and in the end, the eventual cause of what makes us not.

That is why that Nike bag remains in my mind. It's what keeps me human.

Postscript: The medical examiner later decided that after 44 days of life, young Rajasthan Haynie may have been suffocated accidently. So even though the ME confirmed that the baby had signs of trauma to the head and damage to his lungs, the ruling allowed Lakesha to plead guilty to involuntary manslaughter and receive a 10-year suspended sentence.

She was freed in January 2010.

CASE FILE 8

Sewell's Brother

As I've said a number of times before in this book, one of the worst parts of my job as a homicide detective is having to tell a mother her child is dead. There is no sound more horrific than the scream of a mother when she learns that her son has been shot in the back of the head and is lying on a gurney in the morgue.

But even though I have brought bad news to countless families and done my best to comfort dozens of grieving relatives, I never thought I would have to knock on the door of my own mother's house and tell her one of her children had been shot and may not live to see another day.

I'll never forget the night when I entered Johns Hopkins Hospital, suspecting in the back of my mind it was my brother in the ICU fighting for his life.

I had just received a call from an Eastern District shooting detective, Joshua Ellsworth. They had transported a man named Clinton Anderson to Intensive Care.

The victim had been shot in the head and left to die on the 2000 block of East Hoffman Street. Detectives said they had possible witnesses.

And then there was one inescapable detail that forever changed my life. The man lying on the operating table with a bullet hole in his temple was in fact my brother.

A child from my mother's marriage to another man, Clinton was no different to me than the rest of my family. And of course, like any good mother, all of her sons were loved just the same.

So when I knocked of the door of my mother's West Baltimore home, it was, to say the least, surreal.

I know the routine when I knock on the door of a family I don't know. It's not callousness that gets me through it, just a sense that I have a job to do, a painful but necessary job that I try to do as professionally as possible.

I try to get through the door before all hell breaks loose. I try to sit the mother down. I try to say a few words before the grieving begins, even though it's difficult to get a word in once they learn I am a homicide detective.

But with my own mother? All the space between me the detective, and the victim's family evaporates when it's your own family. The wall you create to deliver the news to bereaved relatives again and again as professionally as possible just doesn't work.

When it's your own mother on the couch sitting across from you and your own flesh and blood in the hospital it's just not possible to draw any lines. It's just a mother and her son, and in the end, nothing but pain.

So when my mother opened the door I really didn't know what to say.

"What is it, Kelvin?" I remember her saying. "What's wrong?"

"Sit down mom," I said. "It's about Clinton."

And then it started, she started, because like any other mother she could read her son like an open book.

She knew something was wrong.

"What happened? Tell me. What happened to Clinton?" she demanded, gasping.

And then I told her. I told her Clinton had been shot in the head, that he might not make it, and that we didn't know who did it.

And then my mother, like all the other suffering women I had delivered bad news to, broke down.

Sitting in the living room I felt like a man in between two worlds. I knew the drill; I knew how to build a wall, how to fill the void with conversation. But this time I was speechless, it was my mother after all.

So I just held her and acted like a son. What else could I do? Later I went to the hospital.

Again it was something I'd done a hundred times. Check on a shooting victim on the verge of death. Talk to the doctors. Obtain a prognosis. And wait.

But this time the feeding tubes, the whir of the heart monitor, the death glow of the EKG was all coming from the body of my brother.

I know this sounds odd, as if it's some revelation that the people I see every day are human, like the dead bodies in the morgue that pile up in a holding pattern like so many grounded airplanes outside the main examination room.

But the truth is, the truth that homicide detectives know but will never talk about, is how we really make it through the day. How we see through the corpses and the tortured faces of family, twisted in pain over the violent death of a loved one.

We do it by summoning a sort of benign detachment. Don't get me wrong, I take all my cases personally, I work hard to bring closure to the families who suffer.

But I deal with death, the worst sort of violent death every day, particularly in Baltimore, where the homicide rate is among the highest in the nation.

And the truth is, I couldn't do it without a bit of a wall. A respectful wall, an honest wall between me and the dead, the families, the suspects. A wall built on the vague sense of "the other": the other who suffers, the other who lies dead behind a stone wall in Baltimore's ad hoc "cemetery" on the cusp of Leakin Park.

That other never becomes you. Never assimilates into your reality. You'll never get shot in the back of the head. Your leg will never twist behind your shoulder after you've jumped from the ledge of a bridge. Your face will never be torn apart by animals after someone strangles you and leaves you for dead in the woods.

You won't die alone, left on a sidewalk to be carted to the morgue while a detective lifts your fingerprints from your necrotic fingers.

The twain shall never meet.

But in the hospital that night that wall for me disappeared. My brother was dying, a victim of the same senseless violence I fought to curb regularly, but never seems to end in this city.

I later learned that the shooting, like much of the violence that occurs in Baltimore, was over something trivial.

My brother had been gambling with a group of friends outside his home on Hoffman Street. It was a dice game. Someone got angry, someone opened fire. All over a dice game and now my brother lay dying.

I'm not going to lie, my brother had issues. He battled cocaine addiction and had trouble holding a job. But he was an amiable person. Always smiling, had few enemies, not someone who caused trouble or took his frustrations out on the innocent or weak.

He was, in a sense, like a lot of people in Baltimore; for whatever reason, never really getting their lives on track. Always sidelined by either personal problems or a predilection for substances that ease the pain of trying to get by in a world where the future has little bearing on the problems of the present.

The worst part for me was learning the reason that my brother lay now, connected to a respirator, wasting away inside a hospital.

According to several witnesses a two-bit drug dealer nicknamed "Snake" became angered over a $2 bet. The argument erupted quickly and was over in a minute, whereupon Snake put a gun to my brother's head and pulled the trigger.

After the shooting, Snake and several other men participating in the game fled. But thanks to several witnesses and the good work of Detective Joshua Ellsworth, Snake was arrested and charged with first-degree attempted murder and was eventually sentenced to 20 years in prison.

Still. No matter how much time Snake does, my brother will always be limited by the brain injury inflicted by a single capricious gunshot.

For months he could barely speak. He had to learn how to talk and read all over again. He couldn't recognize members of his own family. He lived in the shadows of traumatic brain injury, a shell of the man I knew, who wasted away inside a nursing home while trying to re-learn the alphabet.

He endured months of physical therapy and additional operations. He was seen by doctor after doctor.

And even after years of medical care and years of therapy he will be unable to work or live independently for the rest of his life.

He is a permanent invalid.

Clinton is one of hundreds of gunshot-wound victims who survive, albeit never really whole again. People whose bodies are shattered in a second but then must live with the horrible consequences for years.

To this day he struggles to speak and interact with his family, and to this day my mother has never recovered from the shock of learning that her son was almost taken from this world because of the split-second irrational decision of a lowlife drug dealer.

I guess to a certain extent it's the price every one of us who lives in this city pays every day for the senseless violence that surrounds us. The wounds never really heal. The pain never really goes away. The lingering aftereffect of the bad decisions people make on the street. The split-second acts of random and unnecessary violence that we all pay for, year in and year out, decades later.

All over two dollars, all because of a dice game.

I know this, not just because I am a homicide detective, but because it happened to my brother.

CASE FILE 9

Failed Suicide

If you think death isn't funny, you haven't been around it long enough. Even in our last moments on earth, we don't lose our sense of humor. Or perhaps it would be more accurate to say, even in death we rarely escape irony.

Of course, people about to die don't necessarily have a joke in mind when they stand on the precipice of a bridge in West Baltimore, staring down at oblivion some hundred feet below.

But how else can I explain the sequence of events that led to two men at the same bridge at almost the same time hell-bent on taking their own lives as quickly and violently as possible.

And I should add, they tried to pull this off from the same spot less than an hour apart.

I have occasionally in this book tried to give you a sense of how absurd things can get in a dysfunctional city like Baltimore. But this one takes the cake.

We had been called to a bridge overlooking a gully on the eastern side of Leakin Park to investigate a suspicious death.

The bridge, on Hilton Parkway, was a favorite spot for jumpers.

When we arrived, sure enough we found the body of a man on the rocks, that had all the telltale signs of someone who had died in a fall. His head was cracked open like a coconut, his one leg twisted nearly behind his head in such a manner that could only have occurred from a violent, high speed impact.

So all the indications were he jumped to his death.

Still, we decided to drive up onto the bridge to have a look.

The idea was to check to see if the jumper on the rocks below leapt from the bridge, based on where he landed. It was just a matter of angles, a visual confirmation to make sure he was at the very least a jumper, not simply another body dropped in one of Baltimore's favorite impromptu graveyards.

What happened next, to this day I still can't rightly comprehend.

As we pulled up onto the bridge overlooking the park, I saw something unusual.

A man was standing next to the railing looking out over the park. Suddenly he started to take off his shirt.

I looked at Detective Joon Kim who was sitting next to me in our 1998 department-issued Chevy Cavalier.

"This can't be happening," I said to him.

It looked like, at least from my vantage point, we had another jumper.

Seriously, while the body of one man was lying on the rocks below, another man was getting ready to jump off the same bridge.

Unreal.

Kim and I got out of the car quickly.

As we approached, the man had finished taking off his shirt and was climbing onto the railing.

"Sir, can I talk to you?" I said to the man.

"Leave me alone," he replied, his eyes bulging out of their sockets, his hands gesturing wildly.

"Just let me talk to you for a second," I repeated.

"Leave me alone, man," he said as he began to climb up onto the railing.

Trying to distract him, I asked.

"Do you want a cigarette?"

He looked at me for a second. His eyes were strained and bloodshot. His face was sweaty, even for a summer day.

Police officers try to pretend they're trained for any situation. It's an air that more than a few professionals, like doctors and lawyers, carry as a crutch. You want people to think you're prepared to handle anything, even when you're improvising, which is what I was doing at that particular moment.

Seriously, a man getting ready to jump from the same spot another man jumped from less than an hour before, how do you prepare for that? What do you say? "Look over the railing, somebody beat you to it"?

With the way things were going, the next thing out of his mouth might have been "I don't smoke."

Luckily, that's not what he said.

"Sure," he replied.

Next I turned to Detective Kim.

"Kim, give me a cigarette."

Kim checked his pockets.

"I don't have any, Sarge."

Now, let me make it clear that Kim was a heavy smoker, had been throughout his entire career in Homicide and for as long as I knew him. Had never known him not to have a pack in hand.

And now, as I stood on the bridge trying to talk this guy down, Kim had decided to leave his pack of cigarettes in the office.

I had to think fast, keep the potential jumper's mind fixated on the idea that he would in fact be momentarily smoking a cigarette.

"I think you left them in the car," I told Kim.

"You may be right," he answered, turning to walk back to the car.

With Kim en route to retrieve what was a nonexistent pack of cigarettes, I had to act.

The distraction wouldn't last, I knew, and soon the man might be over the railing, joining his fellow Baltimorean on the rocks below. He was shaking, and he seemed to be a bit delusional, or high, but certainly not in a right-thinking state of mind.

So I simply had to make a quick decision. As soon as he looked away, as soon as he took his eyes off me, I would take him down.

And sure enough, as Kim neared the car, the jumper looked back over the railing to the rocks below. I don't know what he saw, maybe the body of the other jumper? but for a moment he hesitated, and I didn't wait for another chance.

I lunged at the jumper, grabbed him around the waist, and pulled backwards with all my strength, trying to get him off the ledge and onto the street.

But for some reason he wouldn't budge.

I don't know if it was a reflex reaction to being pulled backwards, or if he really wanted to step over that railing and end his life. All I know is that the man was not going down easy, and I was there on the edge of the railing holding on for dear life.

Fortunately Kim had not really walked to the car, knowing full well there weren't any cigarettes waiting in our department-issued death trap of a Chevy Cavalier. Within seconds he had my back, his hands around my waist pulling me backwards at the same time I was grappling with the jumper who was still giving me a hard time, grunting and breathing but not letting me pull him off the guardrail.

It must have looked like a Keystone Kops impromptu charity wrestling match: I'm grappling with a shirtless man who is trying to throw himself over a guardrail while Kim is grabbing me by the shoulders and pulling me back onto the street. It was a human accordion fronted by two men wearing suits.

Finally, at some point, despite the jumper's best efforts, gravity won out and we all fell backwards onto the street in an unceremonious pile, the jumper on top, Kim on the bottom, and me in the middle.

It was one of those absurd moments in policing, something that no matter how you try to handle it, you can't help but feel like you've landed in the worst possible outtake from Police Academy Meet Martin Lawrence.

What the hell was I doing lying on Hilton Parkway in the middle of the day with a jumper on top of me, a detective under me, and another body sprawled on the rocks below? I remember thinking, is this really happening?

Still, as stupid as it looked to have the three of us rolling on the ground in the emergency lane of a heavily trafficked parkway, I had the jumper in my grasp, and I wasn't letting go.

Kim quickly righted himself and was able to get the jumper onto his feet and in cuffs to make sure he didn't decide to take a second shot at ending his life.

I was slow in getting up: I had heard a pop and felt a sharp pain in my right knee on the way down. I could barely walk.

Meanwhile, a friend of the man we had just pulled off the guardrail showed up and had witnessed the entire sequence of events. He approached Kim, telling us the jumper's name and giving us the phone number of the man's mother.

It was one of the few good-news calls a homicide detective gets to make.

His mother told me her son had recently lost his job, that he was despondent over an ex-girlfriend, and that he had turned to drugs.

Most of all she thanked me profusely; her son was alive, unlike the man who lay dead in the dry stream bed, whose family would soon be receiving a visit from a homicide detective.

I told the mother I was simply doing my job, which was in part true. I investigated a suicide, and ending up preventing a suicide. It was one of those days in Baltimore that show how deep the misery is in this city for the people who have to live on margins.

But it showed too that even when things are bad, the absurd often has a stake in the game.

Even when you think you've figured out why people do stupid things, and why they choose to die by their own hand in a city that offers a million opportunities to have someone do it for them, the absurd steps in and shows you that you haven't got a clue.

That's what I learned when two men decided to jump, that despite our best efforts, the human ability to make stupid decisions will always overwhelm a police officer's ability to figure out why.

CASE FILE 10

MELODY SMITH

Melody Smith

What does it mean to be a cop? And why do we have a criminal justice system at all? Who are we supposed protect? The innocent? the helpless?

That is a question that struck me standing on the sidewalk of the 700 block of Yale Avenue on a hot, blistering spring day in April of 2009. The type of uncomfortable pre-summer furnace particular to Baltimore where the heat-soaked humidity turns the air into a cloying oily skin of smog-soaked water.

We had just been called to a row home in Northwest Baltimore to investigate a suspicious death. Not an uncommon call. People die all the time, and sometimes it just takes an extra few degrees of heat to weaken the body and bring on a stroke or heart attack. But this was not one of those cases.

Inside the home in the living room we found the body of a middle-aged woman named Melody Smith badly decomposed, lying face down on a couch, dressed only in her underwear. She had a wound in the back of her head and had been dead for several days, based on the decomposition that had already occurred.

A friend of the victim, Sheryl Boone, had found the body. Boone was hysterical.

"It was her boyfriend," she told us.

Not just a boyfriend, according to Boone, but a terrorist. A man who stalked Smith at her job with Verizon and prevented her from seeing friends or even taking a trip to the mall. The type of man her friend said beat her regularly, checked her email to search out potential rivals. A man so obtrusive that his prying forced Melody to have items she purchased online sent to a neighbor's address so he wouldn't see them and get suspicious.

In short, he was the kind of man who sounded very much like someone who would kill. And he was nowhere to be found.

As I talked with Sheryl I began to get that sinking feeling in my stomach. The kind that fills a cop with dread. Because as she told me the story of Melody's efforts to call police and get help, I knew where this case was headed.

But more on that later.

The weekend after we believed Melody had been killed, neighbors told us they had seen Gregory Tooson, a Pittsburgh transplant Melody had been dating for two years. He was chatty, neighbors said. Washing her car, asking the neighbors if they'd seen her, all the while her body was rotting away in the living room.

"He was acting like normal," I remember a neighbor telling me. Which is why I started thinking about the whole idea of what it means to be a cop. Why do we police? Who are we supposed to protect?

It's not a trivial question in a city like Baltimore. We do arrest plenty of criminals; we do take violent people off the streets. But we miss some, I think too many.

Because as this case unfolded, what we learned raised doubts in my mind about the whole enterprise of policing in Baltimore. Not the need for it, but the execution. In short, I started to consider the possibility that we had lost our way.

Let me explain.

Tooson was a seriously troubled man. Jobless, several arrests while living in Pittsburgh. He had been violent in previous relationships.

Put simply, he was an accident waiting to happen.

Meanwhile Melody was a quiet God-fearing woman, according to co-workers and friends. A dependable employee who never missed work. A woman who was loyal to a fault. A law-abiding, taxpaying citizen.

From the beginning her relationship with Tooson was tumultuous, her friends said.

He was controlling from the start. Couldn't hold a job. Always short on cash, relying on Melody for money. Dunning her like a collection agent. Borrowing her car and disappearing. He even opened an American Express account with her credit card under his own name, and then tried to convince the bank to deposit her mortgage payment into his account just before he killed her.

And because he was so dependent upon her, he leeched onto Melody, kept her to himself, so to speak.

But as the relationship grew stormier, a clear pattern developed. Melody sought help, mostly from us.

And she was ignored.

When I searched their address for previous police calls — standard procedure for these types of cases — I was stunned. In a little over two years someone at Melody's home on Yale Avenue had called police over 50 times. Not a few, not 10, but 50.

Meanwhile, when I cross-checked to see how we responded to the calls what I found was even more troubling.

Many of the calls to the address had been coded out. The officer who responded had simply reported that an officer was not needed.

No reports filed noting a domestic disturbance, a threat against her, or of violence of any kind.

Not only that, just days before Melody was killed, a police officer did in fact intervene, but not to help her. The officer drove Tooson to the North Avenue Courthouse to help him swear out a protective order against her — a not-uncommon ploy of abusive husbands and boyfriends — after he told police she had tried to attack him with a hammer, which he may or may not have used later to hit her in the back of the head.

In other words, the man who eventually killed Melody was able to get her ordered out of her own home just a few days before he killed her, all with the help of a city police officer.

I remember that same officer showed up at the crime scene when Melody's body was found, nervous and full of excuses. "Maybe it was an accident?" I recall him saying.

"Not a chance," I told him.

I understand that domestic cases are complex. Domestic calls are in fact some of the most dangerous a police offer responds to. When a man and woman fight, there are no winners.

It might seem unfair to blame cops even in part for what happened. After all, we're not social workers. We can't be expected to arbitrate disputes between hostile lovers.

But anyone who thinks there's nothing a cop can do about a man like Tooson doesn't know policing.

Cops have resources. We have domestic violence units that specialize in these types of abuse. An entire division of the State's Attorney's Office that focuses on domestic cases.

We have partners like House of Ruth who can intervene when the officer believes trouble is in the offing. And we have the power to investigate, to figure out just how much threat a man or woman poses to their significant other when a relationship turns sour.

We have all these tools, and yet not a single one was used to help Melody Smith.

Of course for someone like Tooson, the dysfunctional City of Baltimore can be an asset. A place where protocols aren't followed, where police get lazy — and sloppy.

He was, according to several neighbors, a brusque, physically imposing man who could appear friendly just minutes after he was heard threatening Melody inside their home.

A man who could nonchalantly wash the car belonging to the woman he had just strangled. A bum who persuaded the officer responding to the call for help made by Melody, to drive him to court to take out a restraining order, an order subsequently signed by a judge, which forced Melody to leave her own home.

Still, with 50 calls, 50 chances to intervene, somehow someone failed. Not the system, but the people. The culture of policing, our professionalism. The people sworn to protect, did not act.

And Melody Smith isn't the only woman we've recently failed to protect.

Last year the city police admitted to talking no less than 100 women out of reporting they had been raped. Dozens upon dozens of cases that were incorrectly ruled "unfounded."

That's 100 of the city's most vulnerable who were turned away. Incidents that an independent committee made up of women's advocates and medical experts determined were in fact crimes.

Worse yet, we later learned Melody had all but given up on us, or any other agency for help. In fact, if her last few acts upon this earth are any indication, she knew she was going to die.

When my detectives went to confiscate her work computer at Verizon, a FedEx package had just arrived addressed to her. Curious, we took the letter inside the FedEx package along with two other letters found on her desk with her name on them after we obtained a warrant.

The FedEx letter was addressed to her family. Simply put, it said that if she died, that it was Tooson who had killed her. In other words, Smith felt so utterly isolated that she had written a letter and FedExed it to herself at the office. A sort of prior death notice sent from beyond the grave.

With nowhere else to turn, she finally had resigned herself to dying. In a last act of courage, she had decided to insure her killer would be caught.

It was not only heart-wrenching to read the letter, but also maddening to imagine Melody writing it.

What was she thinking as she typed the words that singled out Tooson as her future murderer? How alone and abandoned could this woman have felt? In a city with one of the largest police departments in the country, that managed to arrest nearly a million people in under a decade, a city where police would take people off the street and load them into the back of a van for a so-called "walk through" at the city jail, there wasn't a single cop who was willing to arrest Tooson?

Not a single badge to render Melody aid?

It was depressing to say the least. A victim who cried out for help before the crime. A murder that could have been prevented.

Needless to say we knew from the onset that Tooson was the killer. By the time we arrived, Melody's 2003 Subaru was missing.

The back door of the house, which someone had broken down, had been cleverly put back on the hinges.

We learned that Melody had actually sworn out a protection order against Tooson a day after he obtained his order against her. I can tell you right now that it has become a common tactic for men like Tooson to swear out counter-protection orders; the case files in the basement of the North Avenue District Courthouse are filled with similar files.

But when the hearing was held for both, only Melody showed up. The judge approved hers and found Tooson's without merit, tossing it.

We later speculated Melody returned home after the hearing Thursday. We don't know why. Maybe she thought the order would finally offer her some protection. Maybe she thought, armed with that piece of paper the next time she called the police it would be Tooson who would be forced to leave.

It's hard to say.

But of course none of it helped — because the day after her order was signed Tooson struck her in the back of the head and then strangled her on the couch. We will never know what precipitated the final fight. We will never really know why he finally decided to kill her.

And then he stayed, lingering in the home as I said before. Washing her car and asking neighbors if they had seen her while the body of the woman he had slain rotted on the couch.

I often wonder about people like Tooson. They seem to have no conscience, no soul. What did he do for the three or four nights as he slept in the row home not far from Melody's decomposing body?

Did he sit at the kitchen table enjoying a meal? Did he watch a basketball game? Did he feel remorse?

How could he stay in that home, forced to confront both the stench and the decaying reminder of his crime?

How sick can a person — and by extension a society — become?

As I said before, Tooson had a record — several assault and theft charges in Pennsylvania. At least one previous incidence of domestic violence. Still, not the résumé of a man who kills a woman and then lives with her corpse for several days.

It wasn't until I met him one day in prison that I gained at least a bit of insight into the fabric of the man.

While Tooson may have been a sociopath, he wasn't a very imaginative fugitive.

Several days after Melody died he took her Subaru and returned home to Pittsburgh, where he holed up in his mother's house.

It didn't take long for Pittsburgh police to find him. Shortly thereafter he was extradited to Maryland and locked up without bail.

Later I visited him in jail to obtain a DNA swab, meeting him in the Central Booking medical facility. He had refused to be interviewed when he was initially brought to Maryland, so it was the first time I actually saw him up close.

Prison doesn't suit many people, and Tooson was no exception. He looked like an out-of-shape former linebacker, 265 lbs. stuffed into a 5-foot-11-inch frame. Maybe he was more imposing once before, but he now had the bearing of a deflated balloon.

I asked him how he was doing.

"Not good," he said. "They won't let me put on my cream."

"Cream, I asked?"

"For the burns," he said.

I didn't ask how he got the burns. One question might have turned the conversation into an interview which would soon be followed by a call from his attorney. I told him to go ahead and take off his shirt.

When he did, I can't really describe what I saw. Just dozens of welt marks, burn scars that covered his body like twisted, angry rivers. The marks left on a man who had literally been set on fire.

After we obtained the DNA I went back to the office and did a little digging.

Turns out roughly 15 years ago Tooson had abused another woman in Pittsburgh, according to police there. A woman who decided to take matters into her own hands.

One day she had enough, and set his clothes on fire after he hit her during an argument. The flames caused second- and third-degree burns, scars that still looked fresh in the fluorescent lights of the prison medical center.

But Tooson survived, only to kill later. A man who should have been stopped. A murderer who could have been prevented from killing.

Which brings me back to the question of why we police. Why we put on badges every day.

If you paid attention in Baltimore you would think it's to storm into poor neighborhoods and lock everybody up that we can. To massage statistics and downplay sexual assaults. To fight each other even more vehemently than the criminals on the streets.

But even though I raise these questions, I do it because I don't want people to think that's it — that that is all we're about. I've told the truth, the inside details of many of these cases to the best of my ability in this book, with the hope that my candor can bring change.

And believe me, change is what we need in the BPD.

We, as police, are human, and flawed. We make mistakes, we have egos. And in a city like Baltimore, where the power of policing has been unleashed with few if any limits, we have become to a certain extent accountable only to ourselves.

And that's how Melody Smith slipped between the cracks. That's how Tooson was given the opportunity to murder.

Because police in Baltimore are too tied to politics. Because statistics reign more important than our ties to the community. And because our pensions often become more important than our passion for the job.

Most police officers want to be a force for good. Most of us who enter the Police Academy want to help. But we have to be held accountable not just for numbers, but for our behavior in the community. We have to be supported of course, but monitored at the same time.

It's a tricky balance; something that I doubt is even achievable in Baltimore.

But I'm not going to devolve this book into a rant about cops. I'm going to let the victim here have the final word. I'm going to let Melody speak for herself in a way she was denied while she was still alive.

The last words she may have written were in a request for a protective order, an order which was approved but did her little good.

I hope her words have resonance. I hope we remember her. I hope her death continues to remind us of our real job: To defend those who cannot defend themselves.

The following is what she wrote, her plea for help. A plea we all but ignored.

Gregory went into a rage about an email not directed to him with a friend. He suspected me of cheating. I am not nor ever done so. While explaining I was forced to sit on the bed and told to shut up, I'm dead. I grabbed my phone and called 911, while speaking Gregory grabbed phone out of my hand while I was still on the line. Phone was broken. Gregory went downstairs I then put on clothes and ran out my home, walked around the back and got into my car for fear of my life. I had text-msg my best friend and asked if I could come over. Gregory said I ain't going nowhere. While he was downstairs I slipped out the door fearing for my life. I never touched the hammer.

CASE FILE 11

Hopkins Shooting

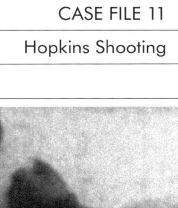

Paul Pardus

There is an indelible sense of truth that pervades the scene of a homicide.

As a detective, the first time you lay your eyes on a body there are clues that immediately catch your attention. Shell casings for example, the location and size of the wounds.

But what really defines a crime scene is the sense of finality that pervades it.

Because even the worst scenes of death and destruction are a composite picture of the last moments of a person's life that can and never will be altered.

Their last act in a sense, fighting to survive perhaps, or caught in the back of the head, unaware, by a bullet. It is the final imprint of that soul upon this earth, and in that sense no matter whose body lies prostrate on the ground there is an aspect of solemnity to each and every murder scene.

With that finality comes a duty to tell the truth about what happened, how that person died. It is like an unspoken oath, a compact between the victim and detectives, that we will get it right, to make sure that each and every detail that we tell the family, and finally the public, is accurate.

To get this part wrong, to even casually release details about a murder — details that may be inaccurate — is a violation of that implicit trust. A slap in the face to the family of the victim, and in the end, the community, the people that we serve.

It can also be dangerous.

I've always tried to stick to that sense of obligation in my career. As much as possible, I've done my best to talk only when I knew in my heart that what I was saying was one hundred percent right.

That's why, when I stood in Room 873 of Johns Hopkins Hospital in September 2010 I was stunned. It was a day of realization for me.

Because on that day, as the whole world watched, the Baltimore City Police Department had given not just the city, but the world, the wrong information about how someone died.

On the floor of Hospital Room 873 lay the body of 50-year-old Paul Pardus, a .32-caliber pistol in his hand, a spatter of blood on the floor where a bullet had exited his head.

Lying in the hospital bed was his 84-year-old mother, Jean Davis, who moments before he had shot and killed in what we could only guess was a state of despair over his mother's condition.

Undergoing emergency surgery was Dr. Richard Cohen, a surgeon whom Pardus had shot after becoming agitated over the outcome of his mother's spinal surgery.

A shooting that was literally heard 'round the world.

A doctor at one of the most prestigious hospitals in the world had been shot in the stomach and was fighting for his life. The entire hospital had been locked down, and the whole world was watching.

And now I was standing over the dead body of Paul Pardus, and staring up at the television set in the hospital room of his mother.

It sounds odd, I know, and insensitive. Why would I be watching television, with a tragic scene of bloodshed sitting literally at my feet? Why would I be staring at a TV screen when all around me was death, another violent end in one of the country's most violent cities?

Because truthfully I couldn't believe my eyes.

Maybe it was a message, or some sort of sign from above? A little prodding or a stark reminder of the odd way the Baltimore Police Department handles a crisis.

But what I saw on the screen that afternoon still perplexes me to this very day. It was sadly ironic that the television in the room was set on CNN. I don't know if Ms. Davis had been watching it prior to the shooting, or a cop had simply turned it on afterwards to monitor the coverage of the shooting. But whatever the reason, I have to think there was one.

For at the moment I was standing amidst the aftermath of a murder/suicide, CNN was reporting a very different story. City Police Communications was telling the national media that we, the Baltimore Police, had shot and killed Pardus. That a police officer had gunned him down.

And they were telling the entire world.

So I stood there looking at the ticker that scrolled along the bottom of the CNN screen claiming that we had shot him, and wondering, How could anyone come to this conclusion? How could such an out of whack story find its way from this hospital room to the rest of the world without someone — anyone — saying, Wait, is this correct?

Perhaps you're wondering why this matters, why an error like this, in the heat of the moment is so important. After all, it doesn't really matter how or why Pardus died, does it? At that point all that mattered was, the threat was over. Right?

Wrong. Dead wrong.

Because what the error represents is not a small lapse in communication, an insignificant type of slip where a suspect's age is transposed, for example, or a time of arrest is off by an hour or so.

When a police department releases inaccurate information on a case where someone died — that was receiving national attention — that type of error hints at other deeper problems.

Remember, the suspect, Pardus, was lying on the floor with a gun in his hand, a close contact wound that indicated suicide. His mother lay dead in her bed, a nimbus of blood spread from the base of her skull onto the folds of her pillow.

So how exactly, with the world watching, did Baltimore City police get this one so wrong? Why was I standing over the scene of an obvious murder/suicide while CNN was reporting that police shot a man who had clearly killed himself?

This is not an easy question to answer, but it is something that speaks to the nature of the Police Department itself, of our ability to handle a crisis.

For that day, the day of the shooting, behind the scenes was nothing short of chaos.

Bear in mind chaos is a natural state of affairs when a man decides to shoot a doctor in a prestigious hospital in the middle of the day. It's certainly not a routine shooting, even in a city as violent as Baltimore.

But it's chaos that a major metropolitan police force is supposed to be prepared to handle. In fact, given the department's emphasis on tactical units and urban pacification, it seems that the Hopkins shooting was a perfect scenario to prove that millions of dollars of grant money expended on our readiness was worth it.

But as with other aspects of the BPD, what goes on behind the scenes is often quite different from what the public hears and sees. Only in this case, the misinformation left a big obvious clue as to what was really going on.

But first let me fill in some of the details of what led up to that moment of realization in Room 873.

According to our investigation, Jean Davis, Pardus's 84-year-old mother, was suffering from debilitating back problems.

A week before the shooting, Dr. Cohen had performed unsuccessful spinal fusion surgery. Apparently Ms. Davis had been suffering from long-term chronic pain in her lower back. The surgery was intended to fuse vertebrae connected by the thorax to the sacrum, a part of the pelvis.

Unfortunately, the operation did not go as planned, and Ms. Davis had to undergo a second operation several days later.

The day of the shooting, Dr. Cohen had just informed Pardus that his mother would not recover and that her prognosis was poor. The doctor told Pardus that he should seek hospice care for her.

And that news, witnesses reported, set him off.

Witnesses said Pardus shot Dr. Cohen once in the stomach, then retreated back inside his mother's room. Alert nurses closed the door to the room and began locking down the floor while a city police officer working off-duty security at the hospital alerted our tactical squad, better known as a SWAT team.

Shortly thereafter the tactical unit responded, locked down the entire hospital, and eventually learned that the suspect was lying dead on the floor.

Which leads back to me and my squad standing over the body of Paul Pardus, watching reports on the news that we had in fact shot him.

One of the first things you learn as a cop is if you don't know, keep your mouth shut. And like I said before, making sure you know what happened before you make it public is even more important.

So because our Communications Department released this misinformation, I was standing there totally confused. What was the motive? What was the point?

And worst or all, the entire world was watching.

Perhaps the behind-the-scenes chaos had a lot do with why, even amidst a preponderance of evidence that a murder/suicide had occurred, the city police spokesman told the world we had shot the perpetrator.

When my squad first arrived at the crime scene, members of the city's tactical unit were in the room, having just cleared it.

But shortly thereafter cops from all over the city started showing up. Pretty soon it got out of control. Everyone wanted to visit the site of the city's most famous shooting, including the top brass and commanders from districts all over town.

And this chaos was not limited to Room 873.

Whenever police respond to what we call an "active shooter" situation in a high density urban area like the Johns Hopkins Hospital complex, one of the first things we do is set up a command post, a single nexus where responding officers can receive coordinated tactical commands. The point is to have one "nerve center," so to speak, to ensure that police on the scene are properly synced to keep everyone safe.

But at Hopkins Hospital that day, there wasn't just a single command center: as far as I could tell there were three. One command center was located on the eighth floor of the hospital, another in a security center on the first floor, and a third on the street, around the corner from where the shooting occurred.

And the lack of centralized command had near tragic consequences.

The only eyewitnesses to the shooting — two nurses — were led straight across the parking lot in front of the building, within the line of sight of the shooter before we knew he had taken his own life. A major mistake that put their lives at risk; a major error and violation of basic police work.

If he had still been alive, because of this miscue he would have had ample opportunity to eliminate a witness with a single shot.

Next of course, were the aforementioned conflicting reports of who shot whom — bad information that could have had deadly consequences.

If the lines of communication were so blurred, what if we had released erroneous information that was even more consequential? What if instead of telling the world we had shot him, we had said the gunman was still alive, on the loose, on the streets, or armed and dangerous in an elevator?

What if we had misled the public — or worse yet other cops, who have to make life and death decisions in an instant — that he was in the lobby, or roaming the hospital looking for new victims?

What if, for example, this bad information had been transmitted amongst the troops, along with an inaccurate description that led to our shooting the wrong person?

Improbable? Not really.

Think about it. If you're a cop on the scene, you rely on information from command, and if command is wrong then your life-or-death decision could be based on faulty premise. That's a simple recipe for disaster.

If, with a mountain of evidence that a murder/suicide occurred, you release a completely inaccurate depiction of what happened, anything is possible.

Seriously, how could the department get something so important so wrong? And who exactly told our Communications staff that this false scenario had occurred? And why did they believe it was credible?

Not a single fact concerning a homicide should be released through official channels until it has been checked. Barring unintentional errors, nobody should have spread that type of false information about a highly volatile and still-changing crime scene.

One of the most essential and potentially deadly sources of error in policing is poor communication in fluid situations such as this. These types of miscues, the failure to relay accurate information to police on the scene, can be deadly.

Just look at what happened at the shooting outside downtown Baltimore's Select Lounge six months after the Hopkins incident. Police Officer William Torbit was killed, shot over 20 times by our own officers, who it seems did not know he was on the scene or what he was doing.

Maybe there was nothing that could have prevented the bloodshed that included the death at that same scene of another young man, named Sean Gamble, plus the shooting of three other bystanders by police. But the fact that it appears the officers shot Torbit leads one to conclude that no one knew he was on the scene at the time the shooting occurred nor was anyone able to differentiate between bystanders and criminals.

This is why I was so stunned at Hopkins, not so much about the inaccurate report itself, but what it implied about our ability to communicate effectively with each other.

Needless to say the truth eventually came out, and after nearly half the force had visited the crime scene we were able to confirm that Pardus had indeed killed his mother and then himself. But the miscues didn't end there.

For some reason a high level commander insisted we bring the nurses who originally identified the shooter back into the crime scene to confirm the identity of both Pardus and his mother post-mortem. This was something that could have been easily accomplished with pictures, for example — if it was even necessary at all.

I tried to reason with the commander because I knew these two women had already been traumatized. But to no avail; the commander insisted.

Following orders, we led the two women into the room, where the body of Pardus, along with brain matter and blood, still lay on the floor at the end of his mother's hospital bed. Ms. Davis was on the bed, her final resting place, the blood-soaked pillow still in place.

As a homicide detective you get used to scenes like this — not comfortable, but simply accustomed. But the two nurses, as much as they work with death every day, were in no condition to have to deal with the shock of having to see both bodies, and in a sense, relive the traumatic crime.

But that is what we were ordered to do, against all logic and reason. Why do it? I asked the commander, when we don't have to. But he didn't reply, simply ordered me to comply with his directive.

So we escorted the two women, heroic nurses who had probably saved other lives that day, into the room. And just as I predicted, all hell broke loose. The women, who had hours before risked their lives by locking down the rooms of other patients when Pardus was still alive and toting a gun, were now in hysterics, forced to relive a crime just hours after it happened.

And as I expected, they screamed and left the room in tears. Later I heard they were so scarred by the experience of having to view the bodies that they were having trouble returning to work.

I can't say this for sure, but this may have been the final straw for me as a Baltimore City police officer that week. Maybe at that point the impetus to retire began to grow.

Because if there's one thing that cops need in order to be good at their job, and to survive, it's common sense, something that I believe we lacked on that day.

It's common sense not to release information if you know it's not true. Common sense again to make sure above and beyond anything else that your command and control is organized. And it is common sense not to subject heroic civilians to unnecessary trauma.

But that day the lack of common sense was apparent. Too obvious for my liking. It seemed that the department, in my opinion, had been overwhelmed with too much politics and too little discipline and structure, and had succumbed to disorder and senseless behavior.

Let me say that I love the Baltimore City Police Department, and the City of Baltimore. I was happy serving the citizens of the city and appreciative of the chance to learn and progress as a police officer. I worked with incredible officers who risked their lives every day in ways that often go unreported and unheralded.

But beyond all the seemingly flawed policies and political influences that had hamstrung this department over time, it is the spirit of policing that I think, that day, was most absent and put us most out of whack. Not just operations, or marching orders, but as I said before, the reason we police.

It's something that is intangible and hard to put your finger on, and a sense of mission that I think has been lost to the onslaught of specialized units and the futility of the drug war.

It was something that became apparent to me one of my first days on the job as Lieutenant in the Pocomoke City Police Department on Maryland's lower Eastern Shore, where I took a job shortly after I retired from Baltimore City.

I was standing outside the Pocomoke City P.D., waiting for a car, I think. As I stood there waiting, I noticed someone across the street waving. Instinctively I turned around to see who the person was waving to.

Suddenly I realized the woman was waving at me.

It was an odd feeling. Baltimore Police are so estranged from the community that I automatically assumed when the woman waved, even though she was looking straight at me, that it was not intended for me. It was so unexpected that it took me more than a few seconds to muster the reflexes to wave back.

And it was at that moment that I realized what I missed most of all

about policing in Baltimore, why I was so discouraged after the Hopkins shooting and why it seemed so cruel to make those nurses view the crime scene.

Because in a sense being a police officer seems right when you're part of the community you serve. When the people you are sworn to protect are a part of what you do, it's easy to put on the uniform; in fact you look forward to it.

I know it's not always that simple, that sometimes you have to make the tough calls, and often you have to be a bad guy, even in a tight-knit community, when someone does something wrong.

But it is that sense of connection to the people you serve that I missed. The simple mission of protecting a community that endows what you do with a purpose.

And I know the blame for the distance between the BPD and the community is complex and falls on many shoulders. I know that mass arrests and bad shootings have created tensions, that ripping and running and an intractable assault on drug dealing have widened that gulf.

But at this point I don't really know if I care about placing blame. I just think that we have to take a step back and consider that there is little point in policing against a community. There's really not much hope if the people with guns and badges have little in common with the people that they serve.

That's what crossed my mind when I waved back to the woman in Pocomoke City. It was a good moment: I felt like I was a part of something, a community. That they trusted me.

And now when I look back over the entirety of cases I have discussed in this book and the question I raised at the outset as to why we kill, it seems clearer to me now more than ever. It's not just because we have to kill or because we want to. It's not because some people are simply going to do the wrong thing no matter what.

It's not simply because there are violent drug dealers and corrupt politicians, or a bad school system or crack-addicted parents who just don't care. It's not just because Baltimore is a poor city or even a city without vibrant recreation centers and fancy swimming pools.

No, I don't think it's simply that. I think it's more, something intangible that pervades the city and seems to live in the summer air like a cloud of lingering smog.

Something that causes us not to wave. That puts four cops eating lunch in a booth at Panera Bread surrounded by the world of people they serve, but without a word being spoken between the two.

Why do we kill in Baltimore?

We kill because we are not whole.

THE CAREER FILES

CHAPTER ONE

What It Means To Be A Cop

It's hard to describe the first day you put on a police uniform.

Like any other profession, there's the anticipation of the unknown. What will my first day be like? Will I have a successful career? Will my boss make my life miserable?

Will I like this job?

But when you first become a cop there are also other questions in the back of your mind:

Will I come home safe? Will I make a big arrest? Will I make a difference?

That last question is not something you ask yourself as a cadet, or even as you work your way up from patrol and into the realm of criminal investigation. But maybe it's a question I should have asked myself before I signed up.

But truthfully, how could I have known that chasing down drug dealers and arresting murderers would be the easy part of my job? I never would have imagined the biggest challenge of being a police officer would be dealing with the problems inside headquarters, not on the streets.

As a criminology major at Coppin State University, an historically black college in Northwest Baltimore, my plan was to join the FBI when I graduated. The idea of being a federal agent was a life-long dream.

However one day during my senior year in 1988 a friend asked me to drive him down to Baltimore Police headquarters, and the rest, as they say, is history.

His name was Van Johnson, one of my classmates at Coppin.

Van was already a Baltimore Police officer. Many times he would come to our criminology class in his uniform, often leaving to go out on a call and then returning. I have to admit, as a young man getting ready to graduate I thought what Van did was pretty cool.

That's why when he suggested I take the police entrance exam while he finished up some business at headquarters, I didn't really hesitate.

When I learned that I had passed and was offered a job in the department, I began to reconsider the idea of joining the FBI.

First, I had met a woman who I wanted to marry. Her name was Rhonda Matthews, a nursing student at Coppin State who eventually became my wife.

I'll never forget the day during my senior year when she looked at me and said, "Are you ready to get serious about your life?"

She also didn't want to relocate every three years, the average time between reassignments for an FBI agent. I could only imagine the toll constant relocation would have on a young family.

So with my future and my soon-to-be wife in mind, I accepted a job with the Baltimore Police Department.

Which brings me back to the day I graduated from the Police Academy.

I'll never forget standing outside the old Police Academy with my classmates Andre Hill, Lester McCrea and Lenny Willis, all of us newly sworn Baltimore City Police officers. All of us filled with a sense of optimism and bravado of being both young and ambitious. We talked about our plans, how we would arrest anyone who broke the law.

Little did I know my first assignment would give me plenty of opportunities to do just that — make arrests.

Straight out of the academy I was detailed to Baltimore's Eastern District, one of the most dangerous precincts in the city. Impoverished, overrun by drug dealers and littered with abandoned homes, the Eastern District was a rough place for any rookie to cut his teeth.

Honestly I had no problem with the assignment. I had plans, I wanted to be in the thick of it; I knew the quickest way to learn was to take on the worst the city had to offer.

And it didn't take long for me to see action.

My first night on patrol I was given a set of keys to a patrol car and a radio, with two simple instructions:

"Don't get lost, and don't get captured."

My first assignment was the 311 post, one of the most dangerous sectors of one of the most dangerous districts. The post was home to some of the most notorious open-air drug markets in the city, a sector known for violent crime, drug dealing, and homicides.

At the time, I didn't know my sector was one of the worst, although I noticed the other officers on my shift whispering to each other, probably speculating on whether the rookie fresh out of the academy could survive the shift.

Still standing in the parking lot of Eastern District station, I didn't have a second to worry about how tough my post was or even to strap on my radio.

Within minutes I received my first call.

I was dispatched to the 400 block of East 20th Street for a burglary in progress. Full of adrenaline, I jumped into my car and turned on the lights and siren, wanting to get to the location as quickly as possible.

It's hard to describe what it feels like rushing to the scene of a crime in progress, especially for the first time. On the one hand, your heart is pumping and your mind is racing. Yet at the same time, as a rookie you're trying to review all the things you were just taught at the academy.

But sort of like playing a sport, once the game starts, it all comes down to instinct.

The first thing I did when I arrived at the scene was to cut my lights and siren, parking a few blocks away — I wanted the element of surprise. It was an abandoned house. The front door was open.

Quietly I crept inside, following the sound of voices. Turning around a corner, I came upon two men removing copper pipes. Later I learned they were area junkies taking the materials to sell, and of course, buy drugs.

Sadly this is the root of most crime in the city, a perpetual cycle of criminality fueled by addiction. It is an unending cycle of despair and self destruction you witness firsthand as a police officer everyday. After awhile you come to realize a million police officers standing on every corner cannot stop it.

But more on that later.

I drew my department-issued Smith & Wesson and ordered the two men to drop to their knees and freeze. Surprisingly, they complied without incident.

So there I was, standing in an abandoned row house a few minutes into my first shift as a police officer, and I was already pointing a gun at two suspects. This is too easy, I thought.

Seconds later, a veteran police officer, Terry Love Sr., who later became a close personal friend of mine, showed up on the scene and handcuffed the duo.

"You got your first felony arrest your first five minutes on the streets. Congratulations," he said.

"Okay," I thought, what do I do now?"

Back at the station, I filled out the paperwork for the charging documents. It's a side of policing they rarely show on television, but actually one of the largest and most important parts of a police officer's job.

Everything we do, every move we make, so to speak, has to be documented. The documentation of a felony arrest can take hours; a shooting, an entire shift. A homicide case can have boxes and boxes of files and paperwork, all filled out by cops.

The reason I mention this now, is because later in this book good documentation will play a crucial role in my battle with the department over discrimination. The rule I always lived by as a cop, and a proviso I would recommend to anybody in police work: document everything.

Anyway, back to my first day.

As I was walking into the Eastern District station I saw several plainclothes officers dressed in riot gear carrying a battering ram and getting into unmarked police vehicles. They stood out not only because they were in plainclothes, but because they were all white.

Curious, I asked a fellow officer, Robert Basset, who they were.

I recall Officer Basset answering, "That's the Eastern District Drug Unit and they are about to go on a raid."

Seconds later, a black officer came running out of the district station, also dressed in plain clothes and wearing riot gear.

"Who's that, "I asked.

"That's Carl Trogdon, he's in the Drug Unit."

"That's what I want to do," I said.

And from that moment on, my efforts were focused on making it into the Eastern District Narcotics Unit.

However one thing that struck me from the first time I saw the unit in district headquarters was its racial makeup.

I wondered, how could you have a successful nearly all-white narcotics unit in a predominantly black neighborhood? Wouldn't you want a mix of both white and black officers? I grew up in Baltimore City so call me a fool, but a couple clean-cut white guys with crew cuts aren't going to be fooling anybody, let alone drug dealers.

Maybe I was naïve at the time, but it didn't make sense.

Still, my main focus was getting into the unit, not the politics.

First I started writing administrative reports to my major asking to be transferred to the Narcotics Unit. Then, following the advice of Officer Terry Love, I started working hard to make drug arrests.

Working Barclay Street above North Avenue, I started staking out drug dealers in abandoned homes, observing and accumulating firsthand knowledge of the focus of drug activity in the area and the addresses where the drug dealing was most acute.

Then I started writing search and seizure warrants, an unheard-of task for a patrol officer. The warrants led to raids by narcotics officers and some major arrests.

Along with extra investigations, I was making at least four drug arrests per shift. All the hard work started to pay off — in part. I would hear from fellow officers that the Drug Unit was watching me.

But even with my drug arrests piling up, white officers were getting promoted to the narcotics and other specialized units, some of them officers who worked only half as hard as me.

This, I would soon learn, was just the beginning of my education on how discrimination dictated how things were done inside the Baltimore City Police Department.

CHAPTER TWO
Eastern District Drug Unit

Trying to break into Narcotics Unit is not that much different from working to obtain a promotion in any other field: You have to stand out, get noticed.

In policing, that means making big arrests, the big bust, and that means work.

In the last decade, the Baltimore City Police Department became more and more obsessed with statistics, or what I'll call "stat happy," and thus the way we policed narcotics changed.

The department adopted a strategy called "ripping and running." Jump out on the low-level dealers on the corner and make arrests, get your stats, book your court overtime, and move on.

But back when I started my career, making a big arrest was the culmination of street work, knowing your beat, and time. You had to wait, learn and watch, before you could move on the big dealers. Sure, every once in a while you would stumble onto a big bust, but usually the biggest arrests were the result of effort and patience.

And there's a reason we used this type of approach.

I'll discuss later how the war on drugs has become something of an exercise in futility, but as narcotics officers we knew taking drugs off the streets was really a small part of making a neighborhood safer. In the long run our most important task was destabilizing the organizations that arose from the profits of drug dealing.

Coordinated criminality — the hallmark of organized drug dealing — is the biggest threat to public safety, period. It changes the character of the community just like any large and profitable business. Be it a neighborhood gang or a loose association of drug dealers, when the tendrils of a criminal organization take hold in a neighborhood or community, it becomes a threat to all.

Honest business people in the neighborhood are forced, or seduced, into laundering cash, for example. Old men are paid to stake out territory, to be the eyes and ears of local dealers. Whole swathes of the city undergo a transformation as the criminal element rules not just the streets, but how people live. Violence solves disputes, guns are the tools of the trade.

It is similar to what happens when any type of business becomes the employer of first resort in a community. If it's a steel mill like Sparrows Point that used to employee 60,000 people, then citizens learn how to run a blast furnace and make steel. If the distribution of illicit narcotics is the most viable business in the neighborhood, then young men take up the trade of violence, absorbing all the antisocial habits and bad attitudes that a successful drug dealer needs to survive.

Unfortunately while in-depth drug investigations have a much longer positive effect on the neighborhood, they don't have the visceral appeal of seeing a bunch of young dealers rounded up and tossed into the back of a van. That's why the Police Department in the late 1990s adopted the "rip and run" approach. The idea was to temporarily disrupt the business on the corner, collect overtime pay, and send a message that was of course political: we're cracking down.

And while making a lot of aggressive busts looks great on TV and impresses the local councilperson, aggressive ripping and running does little to truly interfere with the underlying business of drug dealing in the long run; it simply reshuffles the corner. That being said, if drug dealing is all the community has, then there is little anyone can do, even police, to make things right.

But more on that later.

It was my goal from the first day I stepped into the Eastern District station and put on a uniform to get into the Narcotics Unit.

I had been working in patrol for eight months in one of the worst sectors of the city, but as I expected, I was learning — fast.

One thing I figured out early on is that catching drug dealers and working narcotics is more of a cat and mouse game than muscle play. Dealers are smart, they're always adapting and learning from what we do. Officers have to respond with new ways of policing to be effective.

And this means, more than anything, a lot of flexibility and improvisation.

Having done my fair share of drug busts in those eight months as a patrol officer, I started to develop my own strategies to get the repeat offenders off the street. The point was to make a good arrest while making a name for myself and get noticed.

That's why when I ended up in court with a dealer who was constantly standing on the corner on my post, I was ready, and what happened on that day jump-started my career in narcotics.

Obviously the bigger dilemma for drug dealers, and nuisance for police, is territory. And in a town like Baltimore, where there are at least 20 so-called "open air" drug markets, staking out territory and servicing customers is both precarious and vital.

For the street cop it also poses a dilemma of sorts: How do you get these guys off the streets in a way that will have a meaningful effect? What's the best way to keep the dealers at bay so they don't completely own your sector?

Rounding them up and hauling them to Central Booking — the preferred method resulting from the BPD's so-called "Zero Tolerance" policy — is sloppy, prone to errors, and not really legal. As far as I know, we still live in a democracy where you need probable cause to arrest someone. It's like casting a big net to land a single fish. Ultimately you end up getting everyone caught up, and many of the wrong people in jail.

The drug dealers understand how to work the system. They know the courts are overburdened. They know minor drug charges are going to get short shrift. And they know how to use all of this to their advantage.

That's why when I was sitting in the North Avenue Courthouse listening to a known drug dealer on my post telling the judge that I was lying, I could hardly wait to state my case.

This was a guy who I had told to get off the corner many times, and even arrested once before to no avail. I told the judge exactly that, but the suspect would have none of it.

"Judge, that officer never talked to me before," I recall him yelling out in court.

But little did he know I had a surprise for him.

"Your honor," I recall saying, "I approach him on the corner constantly and tell him to leave. As a matter a fact, the last time I stopped him I removed his jacket, the one he's wearing now, and placed the date and my initials on the collar tag without him being aware of it."

The judge ordered the bailiff to remove the suspect's coat. Sure enough, my initials and the date were right where I said they would be, on the collar of his jacket. The whole courthouse fell out laughing.

Believe me when I tell you that my little episode in court was the talk of the department. Shortly thereafter I was assigned to the Eastern District Drug Unit, my first narcotics assignment.

As I said before, even though I had been a patrol officer for only eight months, I had learned a lot. I was full of ideas, and was eager to get started.

One of the policies of the Drug Unit's supervisor, Sgt. John Beviliaqua, was that if you got hurt in the line of duty and were out for a week you were dropped from the unit. When I joined the unit Officer Carl Trogdon, who was on medical leave, was replaced with Officer Vincent Moore Sr. Officer Trogdon and Officer Moore were both black, meaning there were two black officers in the Drug Unit when I started.

And it was Officer Moore who introduced me to my first dose of racism within the department.

As I said, I was full of ideas and was eager to start making drug arrests. But sharing all the things I wanted to do with officer Moore did not elicit the type of response I expected.

"Kelvin, do you know why you were brought up here?" he asked me.

"To make drug arrests," I answered.

Vince then laughed and said, "You were brought up here to drive the white officers around in the covert vehicles so they can observe drug activity."

"Why can't they drive themselves around?" I asked.

Vince then explained, "Because they are white and they can't get themselves into the drug areas so they use us to drive them around."

"But I can drive myself around in one of the covert vehicles and make my own observations."

Vince began laughing, as if my statement was so naïve that it was funny.

"They won't let you."

It was a wakeup call to be sure, Vincent was telling me that I was going to be a limo driver, not a cop, the police version of Morgan Freeman in "Driving Miss Daisy."

Still, I was young and wanted to please, so even though the thought of being limited to driving white officers around made me angry, I did what I was told and waited for an opportunity to prove that I could do more.

For several months I served as the chauffeur for three white officers, Officers Timmy Snow, Tom Marucci and Frank Schoff. They would hide in the back of the van and make drug observations while I drove them around the Eastern District.

It was humiliating and depressing, and even to a certain extent disillusioning. You have to understand, we all knew what was going on. If all you did was drive, then you couldn't make arrests. And if the white officers were the only ones making arrests, then they were the officers who would get noticed and get promoted.

Since our opportunities were limited, and everyone in the unit knew it, we were treated like a lesser type of cop. I remember thinking to myself, I can't do this.

Vince and I would have to stand in alleys to observe drug activity and then report back to the white officers so they could write search and seizure warrants based on our observations. I can remember standing in those dark alleys sometimes alone, thinking, "When am I going to get the chance to write a search warrant?"

I went to Vince and told him I couldn't take it anymore. I told him I wanted to write a search warrant and do my own observations.

But one day while standing in an alley making observations, Vince taught me a lesson about policing that is not often discussed, but has a lot to do with the problems I reveal in this book: It's all about the money.

"If they write the search warrants and use our observations, then they go to court to testify as to what we observed," Vince said.

"That's how they get their court overtime."

Thus I learned pretty quickly, when you peel back the layers on many of the issues that hamstring a police department, money, and in particular overtime, is at the core.

Court overtime is much prized within the department. It's easier than working the streets, and if the case gets dropped you still get two hours' minimum overtime pay. The point is, Vince told me, he who writes the warrant gets the overtime. In the end, overtime means higher pay.

That was one lesson that Vince taught me. The other was how dangerous policing can be, and how thin the line is between life and death in a dangerous city like Baltimore, even for people who carry a gun and wear a badge.

One day Vince and I were on our way back to Eastern District station after dropping off drugs we confiscated during an arrest. We were just passing the 1100 Block of Proctor Street when we spotted drug activity.

Vince said, "Let's stop and check it out."

We parked our unmarked vehicle on Proctor Street and got out. But before Vince could step onto the curb, a man with a gun suddenly jumped out of the alley and fired three shots, hitting Vince in the wrist and chest.

It all happened so fast I could hardly process what happened. It's hard to describe. One minute you're driving around talking about a drug arrest and within seconds all the calm and normalcy of the day is shattered by a barrage of bullets. One minute you're talking to an officer you love and respect, and the next he's lying on the ground bleeding from his chest.

I started to chase the shooter down the street. But Vince called for me to come back. So I rendered aid until an ambulance arrived.

Standing over a friend who has just taken a bullet is something you never forget. It's not just the fact that someone you respect and care about may die. Or that within a matter of seconds someone who a moment ago was fine, talking, doing his job, could be taken from this world in an instant.

What struck me that afternoon was how vengeance and malice ruled the streets of Baltimore to such an extent that no one, nobody, could have even the remote expectation of being safe. After all, we were cops, armed police officers, and yet someone was more than willing to ambush us in broad daylight.

Someone was hell bent on killing us, and willing to commit murder over a few words, because it turned out the shooter was upset with something Vince had said to him while we were patrolling the area just hours before.

This is something I struggle with both as a cop and man. Everyone has pride; everyone wants to be treated with respect. But to shoot a police officer, or anyone else for that matter, over a few words?

It's something that happens more often than you think. And no matter how long you work the streets, it's something that is almost impossible to understand.

Later we learned the shooter was a drug dealer named Charles Bradshaw. As I said before, he shot Vincent because of something he said while we were working a drug case earlier in the day on Proctor. Let me repeat that: he tried to murder a police officer over a verbal slight.

We also discovered that Bradshaw had paid our informant $2,000 to drive him to Paxville South Carolina after the shooting. When the informant returned, we paid him $2,000 to tell us where Bradshaw was located.

Bradshaw was then arrested, tried and convicted, and is still in prison, I hope.

After the shooting Vincent left and was assigned to another unit. I continued to serve as a chauffeur for several more months, but after the shooting I knew more than ever that I did not want to waste my time in the dead-end role of a permanent driver, so I left the Narcotics Unit and went back into patrol.

Fortunately for me, a new opportunity was on the horizon which would change my career forever.

CHAPTER THREE

Back On The Beat

Even though I was disappointed with my stint in Eastern District Drug Unit, my first experience as a narcotics officer didn't kill my desire to work in drug enforcement.

As soon as I got back into patrol in the Eastern District I focused my efforts on building a reputation as a good narcotics officer. Simply put, I went right back to what I was doing before, making drug arrests.

One day I was at Eastern District station when I bumped into an officer named Melvin Russell.

"So you're Kelvin Sewell," he said as he introduced himself. "You're the one who's been breaking all my drug records in patrol."

"I've been sent here by my captain," Russell told me. "I'm in a unit called the STOP Squad and we've been hearing a lot about you; and my captain wants to talk to you about coming to the STOP Squad. The captain wants to interview you."

The captain was Ron Daniel, a highly respected commander who would later serve as commissioner for all of 57 days before then-Mayor Martin O'Malley fired him and promoted Ed Norris to top cop in 2000.

Just a side note: It's pretty much common knowledge that Daniel did not want to implement the Zero Tolerance policy that then-Mayor O'Malley insisted on employing when he was elected in 1999.

The strategy called for targeting high-crime areas with quality-of-life arrests for drinking on a stoop or spitting on the sidewalk, a controversial policy that in my opinion got out of hand in Baltimore. By the middle of the decade an arrest became a weapon rather than the end result of a proper investigation. Looking back on all the wasted money, officer time, and lawsuits against the city, I think in retrospect Daniel was right.

Anyway, Melvin told me the STOP squad worked in public housing units throughout the city targeting drug dealers, and that Captain Daniel was interested in speaking with me about joining the unit.

I didn't say anything at first. My experience with the Eastern District Drug Unit had made me wary.

"I won't be driving people around in a covert vehicle, will I?" I asked Melvin. He laughed and said, "I heard about your experience with the Drug Unit here, and believe me, that won't happen in the STOP Squad."

The next day I had my interview with Daniel and within the week I had joined the STOP Squad and was back in narcotics.

The STOP Squad was an entirely different experience from the Eastern District Narcotics Unit. Right from the start I was put to work with good officers, all of us doing what we loved, taking drug dealers off the streets of Baltimore.

In fact, I think we were one of the best units in the city. Just like a good team, we had good chemistry, the right balance of personality and a common love of working narcotics. All the cops were top-notch, having been recruited into the unit for their accomplishments as patrol officers. Everyone stuck together and watched each other's backs. We even socialized after work, which is saying something, considering the long hours a narcotics unit works.

Just to note who was in the squad, out of respect to my fellow officers: Among the best I ever served with were supervisor Sgt. Keith Tiedemann and Officers Melvin Russell, Jesse Oden, Dorsey McVickers, Bob Bigos, Dave Chevront, Mike Crocker and Greg Woodlon.

During my tenure with the STOP Squad I also got to know many of the city's best judges, including John Prevas, who died unexpectedly last fall; John Themlis, Roger Brown and Marty Welsh; first-rate judges all.

One the great things about working with such a respected group of officers, is that when we needed a warrant, any hour of the day or night, on the golf course or in a restaurant, the judges would sign it. They knew the STOP Squad was thorough, professional, and got the job done.

Of course, every unit has its dark side. A bad actor who abuses the power and the public trust that comes with being a police officer.

In our unit, that officer was a woman who I will name only as "CJ" — and her story is both a cautionary tale about how difficult it is to catch a cop who wants to break the law, and how painful it can be when one of your colleagues decides to go rogue and put you in the position where you have to do something about it.

That was the case with CJ. We had all noticed she would often pocket items from crime scenes that were not relevant to the case and would not end up in evidence. It made everyone in the squad uneasy.

One night we raided a row home on the 1800 block of Castle Street, a suspected drug house.

The raid netted a fairly large cache of drugs and money.

After we secured the premises I was designated as the seizing officer, the cop on the scene responsible for counting the money and other valuables and putting them into evidence.

CJ asked me if I needed help counting the money and I told her no. I was already uncomfortable with her obvious penchant for taking things out of crime scenes, so I certainly didn't want her handling money when I was responsible for it.

Still, after the money was counted CJ came back to the table and took one of the packets of money and put it into the pocket of her raid jacket.

Officer Gregory Woodlon, who had been helping me count the money, looked at me and said: "CJ just took some money; and look, Kelvin, it's sticking out of her pocket."

I felt sick to my stomach. One of our own was not only breaking the law, but was flagrant enough to do it in front of all of us.

When I counted the money again, we were $1500 short, the exact amount in one packet.

So we placed the seized currency in the trunk of our car and then reported CJ to our supervisors.

Not surprisingly she flat out denied doing it when confronted.

The next day Greg was sitting at his desk in our office when CJ showed up and dropped a slip of paper on her desk. Curious, Greg took a look, and found a bank deposit slip showing she had put $1400 in cash in the bank.

When CJ saw Greg looking at the slip, she laughed.

"I just got my tax return," she told him.

After roll call, Greg told me what he saw.

"That dumb bitch put the money she stole from the raid last night in her credit union account. I saw a deposit receipt for $1400."

We reported what we saw to Melvin, who wrote it up and sent the report up the chain of command.

Now at this point you're probably thinking, with two officers who witnessed CJ take money from a crime scene and the fairly strong circumstantial evidence of the deposit slip, that it would only take a quick phone call down to Internal Affairs to get an investigation under way.

But all the evidence in the world doesn't matter when it comes to crooked cops. What matters is politics, and to a certain extent, the well-known fact that we're always reluctant, no matter how badly an officer is behaving, to go after one of our own.

It was decided the entire squad would have to take a lie detector test. But as I soon learned in the BPD, even something as routine as administering a lie detector test to a narcotics officer can be complicated.

CJ had well-known routine for avoiding lie detector tests. Almost without fail, she would always get out of it by saying she had premenstrual syndrome, or PMS. Her ruse had managed to help her avoid almost every lie detector test previously administered to the squad.

So her supervisor told the polygraph operator to be prepared for her scheme.

Sure enough, on the day she was scheduled to take the test, CJ said she had PMS. The polygraph operator told her to take a couple days and come back.

Several days later, she showed up again, acting nervous. But this time she was not given an out, and subsequently she failed the exam and was forced out of the squad.

Of course, I make this point and tell CJ's story to illustrate something that will bear on many of the incidents I recount regarding discrimination inside the department.

CJ stole money from a crime scene. Let me put it simply: she committed a crime. She was, according to the law, a criminal. But what happened?

She was transferred to the Southern District and later promoted to Sergeant. That's how it works. That's the essence of the problem. She got away with a crime. How can we expect officers to have integrity, how can we expect a department to uphold the law, if we have criminals in our midst?

There's no gray area on this one. I understand that things can go wrong during a drug raid, or an arrest. But as soon as she picked up that money and walked out, she was a thief. Worse yet, a thief with a badge — who was promoted to the rank of Sergeant, a front-line supervisor.

But CJ's story doesn't end there. Three years later a sergeant called me into his office. He was concerned, he told me, because CJ was about to take over the Southern District Drug Unit.

The supervisor decided to place an anonymous letter under the door of Internal Affairs.

Soon I and every other member of the STOP Squad were interviewed by Internal Affairs. Charges were filed against CJ and she was fired after a Trial Board hearing.

Some time later, in 1993, the STOP Squad was disbanded and I was transferred to Criminal Investigation Division's Drug Enforcement Section, where I teamed up with Officer James Scott to continue work on drug investigations in the city's public housing.

It was working with officer Scott that I planned and executed one of the biggest drug raids of my nascent career.

We had been doing undercover work in the city's Murphy Homes projects in East Baltimore, a drug infested low-income housing complex that was torn down by the city in 1998.

Through our work we had uncovered a fairly extensive drug ring which required 32 warrants to be written as we prepared to conduct a raid. We called it "Operation Good Night's Sleep," an acknowledgement that drug dealing was so rampant in the project that elderly residents could not get a decent night's sleep.

One of the challenges we faced as we put together plans to execute the warrants, was how to get 200 officers into the projects relatively unnoticed. The command authorized us to rent two U-Haul trucks, which we would use to transport the officers.

Just prior to the raid we assembled the 200 officers at the National Guard's Fifth Regiment Armory in midtown. We briefed the officers, telling them our plans to enter the project from behind on Argyle Street.

Once we arrived, officers took positions throughout the complex to watch for people who would throw drugs out the window.

The raid was a complete success: We seized large amounts of drugs and currency. As we sat in our offices writing reports that evening, I remember watching the news.

A reporter was standing outside of Murphy Homes interviewing elderly residents who were praising us for bringing peace to the project. It was a good feeling, to see how policing could improve people's lives and bring about positive change.

Unfortunately it was a feeling that would become less and less common as my career with the BPD progressed.

CHAPTER FOUR

Federal Drug Enforcement Administration

Like every other business, the drug game changes with time.

Before I joined the Baltimore Police Department, narcotics was like everything else in Baltimore, an old-school family business. That's why you have characters like "Little Melvin," the Baltimore City heroin king who played "The Deacon" on the TV show "The Wire."

He was pretty much ingrained into the fabric of the community, even to the extent that he had a well-publicized friendship with former Police Commissioner Leonard Hamm after he got out of prison and gave up dealing.

Of course, I'm not a fan of the man. In my mind Little Melvin was a drug dealer, nothing more. In fact, it says a lot about the City of Baltimore, and the media, that its leaders would celebrate Melvin as a quasi-celebrity worthy of befriending.

My advice to people who admire him is to join me one day when I sit down on some citizen's couch and have to tell a mother that her son is dead. Try it once, and Little Mel won't seem so appealing.

In the 1990s, the drug game changed. Crack cocaine was an explosive new product, and the money it brought into the city's poorest neighborhoods made the business of selling drugs a goldmine for the poor and unemployed.

Anyone who was violent and crazy enough to hold down a corner and move product while not getting killed, could make big money quickly. It was kind of like Silicon Valley during the technology boom but fueled by ramped up narcotics that were highly addictive, cheap, and easy to sell.

That's why I decided to join the U.S. Drug Enforcement Administration, the DEA — because the street game was changing and I wanted to work with the best.

The opportunity arose from a case that can only be described as bizarre.

One day during our normal course of working narcotics, we got a tip about a large amount of heroin, a kilo, at an odd address — a senior citizen building in Murphy Homes, a Baltimore City housing project.

A kilo is a lot of product. You can't move a kilo of heroin in Baltimore without a large distribution network.

The discovery of such a large amount piqued our interest. We seized the heroin from an apartment in the senior citizen building, and then started an investigation. What we discovered solidified in my mind the golden rule of narcotics: Expect the unexpected.

As we interviewed people living there and continued to work undercover during a year-long investigation, we soon learned that a major heroin distribution ring was being run out of the building reserved exclusively for senior citizens. In fact, the ring was a major player in the regional distribution of heroin, with a distribution network that stretched to the Eastern Shore as far as Dorchester and Worcester Counties.

But even more intriguing, this ring was not run by young guns or even middle-aged drug dealers, but by a group which in Baltimore City is as rare as dinosaurs.

This heroin distribution organization was simply a collection of "old heads," a group of half a dozen men in their mid to late sixties who lived in senior apartments in Murphy Homes. Even funnier, these guys were acting like kingpins, keeping girlfriends in their twenties, transporting large quantities of drugs even though they could barely walk — and most of them moving "weight," the Baltimore euphemism for a large quantity of drugs.

When we finally made the bust, it was like something out of a Martin Lawrence comedy, with half a dozen suspects using walkers or in wheelchairs, being loaded into a paddy wagon. It was both the saddest and funniest drug bust in my career.

It was also fruitful — with cash, drugs and even vehicles seized.

When the trial was over, with the suspects convicted, I was working at Baltimore Police headquarters when a special agent from DEA named Larry Hornstein approached me and posed the question every narcotics officer wants to hear: Do you want to join the Federal Drug Enforcement Administration? The DEA.

It was a great moment: My work was being recognized. Better

still, a stint with the DEA meant you had reached the highest level of competence for a narcotics officer.

My first assignment with the DEA was with Group 51, where I was given the title of Task Force Officer.

Group 51 was a multi-jurisdictional task force that included officers from Anne Arundel, Howard, and Baltimore Counties, along with DEA agents and the Maryland State Police.

Our job was to do major investigations and make felony drug arrests in the State of Maryland.

My first partner was Special Agent Terry Loftus. A five-year veteran of the DEA, he was a soft-spoken officer who pretty much kept to himself. I viewed our partnership as an opportunity to both learn and to teach.

He would teach me how the DEA worked, the strategies they used; I would give him insight into the streets of Baltimore.

For four years we worked side by side undertaking major narcotics investigations, and during that time we developed a sense of teamwork that was both productive and exciting. In fact, we became so efficient that the entire unit was riding on our coattails.

We worked several high profile cases, including the Berkley Pollard case, which involved a major drug dealer also known as Tojo.

Tojo ran an influential drug organization that sold crack cocaine on the West Side of Baltimore in the Poplar Grove/Edmonson Avenue area during the mid-1990s.

As drug dealers go, Tojo had a fairly well-structured organization which included two lieutenants, Rodney Smith and Jamaica Jay, both dangerous men who kept control over the territory that Pollard used to move his product.

For this case, I worked undercover as a drug buyer, hoping to work my way into a position to make a major buy.

I know the idea of an undercover narcotics agent is a staple of television crime dramas, the guy with the fake identity who lives the life of a drug dealer, driving spiffy cars and flaunting lots of cash, but who goes too deep and loses his identity along with his grip on reality.

Truthfully that sort of undercover work, if it happens, is not only impractical, but probably not even effective.

Think about it: your job is to get in, find the players, and make a buy. Not to infiltrate the organization to the point that you know everything. More importantly, the best way to infiltrate a drug organization, big or small, is to be a customer, and since there is no group of people more suspicious and paranoid than drug dealers the best way to get it done is to keep it low key.

So that's what I set out to do with Tojo.

First, I used a criminal informant to set up a meeting. I told him to tell Tojo's lieutenant, Rodney Smith, to set up a lunch so we could buy an ounce of cocaine at a restaurant on the West Side.

From the beginning of the meeting, I tried to put Smith at ease, which I accomplished simply by not trying. I didn't say much, just passed $800 in DEA-marked currency to the informant under the table, who handed it to Rodney. Rodney in turn handed the cocaine to the informant, who handed it back to me.

After the deal was done, I asked Rodney if he was hungry. The idea was to hang around, make him feel as ease and perhaps more likely to do business with me directly.

I told a few jokes, basically shooting the breeze with him as we ate. At the end of the meal I achieved my objective: Rodney gave me his direct phone number.

Once I built a buying relationship with Rodney, the investigation took off.

I called Rodney again, this time setting up a meeting for myself and another DEA agent, Stuart Parker, just off Edmondson Avenue.

When we arrived, Rodney was upset. "Who is that?" I recall him asking, warily.

"This is my man Stu," I told him.

The idea was to get Rodney comfortable with Stu so that Stu could makes buys as well and we could build a strong case. After the meeting, Stu started buying directly from Rodney.

We took the same approach with Jamaica Jay.

Using an informant we set up a meeting. After making the first buy through the informant, I started buying from Jay directly. Over a period of several months both Stu and I purchased over a kilo of cocaine.

The problem was that we knew the cocaine belonged to Tojo; he was the head of the organization, and we still hadn't gotten to him.

One day we learned from an informant that Rodney was planning to take a weekend trip with his girlfriend to Freeport, in the Bahamas. During the jaunt, Tojo would be handling Rodney's customers directly.

This was our chance. We had two days to make a direct buy from Tojo, so we enlisted everyone on the task force to work over the weekend.

Tojo had Rodney's telephone, so I organized a surveillance team to set up a controlled call, a phone call made with the purpose of drawing out a suspect who we believed was engaged in ongoing crimes.

To make the call and then buy, we used an undercover Maryland State trooper who I won't name to protect his identity.

I instructed him to call Tojo and set up a purchase of one ounce of cocaine.

When the officer called, Tojo picked up the phone.

"What's up, Rodney," the officer said.

"This ain't no Rodney, this is Tojo."

The call went well, and Tojo agreed to meet the undercover officer at a gas station on Franklin Avenue, just off 5th Street in Brooklyn.

When the officer arrived, Tojo calmly walked over and handed him the ounce of cocaine. Even more to our surprise, Tojo let him know he could deal directly with him in the future.

"Hey man, listen: Rodney be dealing with anybody. You seem cool, here's my personal telephone number. Call me if you need anything else."

We couldn't believe it. It had taken over a year, but we finally had the biggest drug dealer on the West Side in our sights.

But we didn't have much time; we knew through an informant that Tojo was planning on meeting Rodney at the airport to find out who our man was.

On Monday his phone was ringing off the hook. Both Rodney and Tojo were trying to set up a meeting to see if Rodney would recognize him.

But it was too late for them.

We had spent the rest of the weekend writing out search and seizure warrants. Next we assembled the task force, devising a plan to arrest Tojo, Jamaica Jay and Rodney, then seize all of their assets.

The day of the arrests was a major victory for all of us working the case. We seized 13 cars, two businesses, and two boats. During the entire investigation we also seized several kilos of cocaine.

But the biggest success for us was taking the trio off the streets. Tojo, Rodney and Jamaica Jay were convicted in federal court of drug dealing and running a drug organization. They all received lengthy prison sentences.

But with all good things come bad as well. Policing, like many other high profile occupations, is in part driven by ego, and my success working with Terry created some tension with Baltimore County officers on the task force.

Envy is a powerful motivator and toxic ingredient when it comes to policing. I say this because unlike interoffice politics, police have much more potent and life-altering ways to settle a score or take down a rival, a variety of tools that often interferes with good police work and gets in the way of getting the job done.

I'll give you an example, something that occurred shortly after my success with the Tojo case.

I was working undercover in the Mosher Street area in West Baltimore — tracking a drug dealer with the street name "Fryson" — with two white DEA task force officers from Baltimore County who I will not name. I note their color because there is a truism about undercover narcotics that is at the root of the tensions I discussed before.

White police officers, even if they're undercover, have a hard time working the inner city streets of Baltimore.

So when Fryson stopped his vehicle, I exited my car to see what was going on.

As I walked past his beige Bronco, I noticed the middle compartment by the driver's seat rise up, and in it what looked like almost a kilo of cocaine.

Quickly I responded back to my vehicle and called in what I had seen, hoping to make an arrest. But to my surprise one of the county officers told me to break off the surveillance and come back to headquarters.

When I arrived back at the DEA offices, I asked him, "Why didn't we take Fryson?" To which he replied: "We'll get him another day."

It was an odd statement. A good narcotics officer has to be opportunistic. When you spot a drug cache that large in the possession of the suspect you're targeting, 99 times out of a hundred you make the arrest.

Shortly after that incident I was pulled off surveillance on another case and told to report back to the office to conduct an interview.

When I arrived, DEA Group Supervisor Steve Derr was waiting for me in the interview room, along with Fryson. Needless to say, I was surprised.

"Why am I conducting the interview for Denny and Al's case?" I asked, referring to the two officers who had been spearheading the Fryson investigation.

But Steve didn't answer. As I sat down and started to interview Fryson, Steve said he had to take a phone call and left the room.

Once he left, Fryson started talking, but not about drug dealing. Instead, he started offering me bribes, $300,000 dollars to look the other way. I told him I had to think about it, then left the room.

I found Steve and told him what happened. I suggested we play along so we could get him with drugs, money, and the charge of bribing an officer. Steve said he would think about it, while at the same time he appeared to be relieved. I was told to return to surveillance.

What I didn't know at the time but later learned, was that the interview with Fryson was an integrity test. Fryson had tried to clear himself by implicating me with a crime.

The interview room was set up with both audio and video surveillance. The two county officers working with a U.S. attorney had devised the sting in an attempt to catch me.

I will never know what they thought I did, but I can say that Baltimore City police officers rarely get the benefit of the doubt, particularly if they're black. County officers think that we're liars and cheats, and don't trust us, which is why I think I ended up in that interview room with Fryson.

Still, I passed the test and the DEA offered me a job. But it seemed far less appealing to me after that.

Terry Loftus and I had accomplished so much together, yet they still didn't trust me, and took the word of a drug dealer over mine. When I thought about it, I knew that if I stayed in the DEA there would always be officers who wouldn't trust me and make my life miserable if they believed I was a threat.

So I turned down the job and returned to patrol in the Southwestern District. It didn't matter: things were looking up for my career as a city police officer; I was about to be promoted to Sergeant.

Terry later left the streets and became a pilot for the DEA. Much to everyone's dismay, he was killed in the line of duty when a plane he was flying crashed shortly after takeoff from Midway International Airport in Chicago. Terry was working with the DEA's Kansas City District Office at the time of the crash as part of a Title II investigation, transporting evidence to St. Louis when the crash occurred.

It was a major loss for the country and for me personally. Terry was a good and honest officer who worked hard, always giving his best. He had integrity and a sense of duty.

CHAPTER FIVE

Sergeant

It wasn't long before I returned to the Baltimore Police Department that I again encountered the kind of subtle but ongoing racial hostility that seems always to be beneath the surface.

Three months before being promoted to Sergeant, I was assigned to the Southeastern District, which was considered to be one of the best district assignments in the city.

The district was staffed predominantly by white officers.

One day in the parking lot I was stopped by Officer Greg Taylor. We all knew that Taylor didn't like black officers; in fact he did not speak to black officers, as a rule. So when he stopped me in the parking lot, I was quite surprised.

"You're Kelvin Sewell, right?" he said. "Just so you know, you're not getting promoted; they're stopping at me on the Sergeant's list."

I didn't say anything; just waited, thinking to myself, no way he was going to be promoted over me.

And sure enough, when the promotion list came out, Taylor was promoted to Sergeant, but so was I.

Shortly thereafter we ran into each other at Western District station, where I had been transferred. He seemed a little uncomfortable, to say the least. I just shook his hand and said congratulations, not waiting for or wanting to hear his response.

The Western District was staffed primarily by black officers. It was a rough precinct, to say the least.

The first day I arrived I parked my truck literally 10 feet from the district headquarters door on Riggs Avenue. When I returned, my truck had been broken into and my uniform stolen. I couldn't believe it. When I told my major, he didn't seem surprised at all.

"They got you too, huh?"

Then a few months later during a supervisors meeting, the lieutenant was giving us a briefing so we could prepare for New Years Eve. In the Western District, he told us, residents have the strange tradition of shooting guns into the air at midnight. Just as he was speaking, three gunshots rang out right outside of district headquarters.

"Like those gunshots," he said.

I checked my watch, it was only 9:30 p.m., still two and a half hours to go until midnight.

Brazen scofflaws; indeterminate bold theft; shooting in the air to celebrate the beginning of a New Year: This was not the assignment for me. With a background in investigations, I knew right then patrol was not the place I ought to be; I had to get out.

So I asked the major for a transfer and he assigned me to the Western District Domestic Violence Unit.

Domestic violence cases rarely get attention until something tragic occurs. Neither does the work of the Domestic Violence Unit grab headlines like Homicide or Narcotics Division.

But during my brief time as a supervisor, I learned that the work of a domestic violence unit is some of the most complicated in policing; there is a constant tension between trying to enforce the law while mediating the most delicate and often explosive situations.

Many of the cases involve women who are regularly being beaten by abusive boyfriends and lovers. And while my stay in this unit was brief, I learned that poverty and isolation contribute big-time to the abuse of inner city women. Simply put, many of the women who sustain the worst abuse, but who refuse to leave, have little support and nowhere else to go.

But as I said before, my stint in that unit was brief; things were changing quickly in the department. The "New York Boys" were coming.

When now-Gov. Martin O'Malley was elected Mayor of Baltimore in 1999, he promised to reduce the homicide rate below 200 from the then-average toll of over 300 killings per year. Basically he staked his career — and his political future — on his ability to reduce crime.

O'Malley decided that it was up to the Police Department to help him keep that promise. Thus the BPD and O'Malley's political future became intertwined.

Now I understand why you might be thinking, What's wrong with using the Police Department to reduce crime? Isn't it the job of police to stop crime?

Well, yes... and no.

It may sound stupid, but O'Malley's decision represented a big philosophical change in how we had policed the city. He wanted us to prevent crime, and to be exceptionally proactive in preventing violence.

Technically there's nothing wrong with the idea; however police in a democratic society can't simply pull people up because we think they're about to commit a crime. Or stop them and incarcerate them for what we think — or even know — they might do. In general, and I'm saying this with a bit of irony, someone has to commit a crime first before we can do anything about it.

From that departure point the Baltimore Police started doing things that are both examples of bad policing and unconstitutional activity — like making thousands of illegal arrests.

In fact, Baltimore City arrested so many people during that period that roughly a quarter of all the arrests ended without charges, a number which hurt our efforts to fight real crime, and put us at odds with the community.

In the beginning the new ideas held promise when O'Malley brought in former New York Deputy Police Commissioner Ed Norris to run the department.

Norris was a no-nonsense cop, and a good leader. As soon as he took over, things changed. All the district detective units were taken out of patrol and run through a centralized criminal investigations division, for example.

Because I had a great deal of investigative experience, I was transferred out of the Domestic Violence Unit and placed in the District Division Unit, which handled shootings, robberies, and domestic violence under one umbrella.

Almost immediately word came down from the new leadership that District Division supervisors should send a list of all the equipment we needed to run our units effectively. So I spent hours compiling a list of computer equipment, cellphones and cars that I felt the unit needed. I submitted the list and waited.

Nothing happened.

After several months I realized the apparent changes to the department that were being so heavily touted in the press were somewhat superficial.

One day Jack Maple stopped by Western District headquarters. Maple was the brains behind COMSTAT, "computer statistics"-aided policing. He had developed the idea in New York of mapping out crime trends using computers and allocating resources based on the results. The idea was credited as being new and innovative and with reducing crime in New York City.

I don't know for sure if this is true, but in my opinion, from that success grew many police strategies that can be equally as harmful as they are productive, like the failed arrest policy.

Still, it was Maple's job to bring this idea to Baltimore. He was touted as a genius of sorts.

So when he stopped by Western District, I quickly printed out the list of equipment I had requested and handed it to him.

To my disappointment, he expressed disinterest in my equipment list, even to the point of being dismissive of it. Thus I immediately realized that the promised great change to the department was significantly less than substantive.

Shortly thereafter I was transferred to Internal Affairs, a change in jobs that would significantly alter the path of my career.

CHAPTER SIX
Internal Affairs

In the summer of 2000, I was transferred to the Baltimore City Police Department's Internal Investigations Division.

Let me say this first about Internal Affairs: The IID division in the BPD was the equivalent of the mailroom. Vital to the functioning of the agency, but pretty much ignored as a backwater assignment.

Part of the reason is that the BPD, like every police department, is incestuous, only more so. Most of the internal charges generated inside the agency are the result of turf wars, personal vendettas, or command beefs between officers who are out of favor.

So when I was assigned to IID, I wasn't too excited. Running integrity tests was not exactly the way to make friends, let alone advance your career.

The job was fairly easy for me. Drawing on my experience in Narcotics, I already knew some of the officers with questionable character. We also had a new chief of Internal Affairs who couldn't investigate her way out of a darkroom. But still, Commissioner Norris seemed committed to improving the effectiveness of IID, so I went to work designing and planning integrity tests.

My first day at IID was a bit of a shock. Once I arrived, I was put in charge of a squad with eight detectives. But I soon learned there was very little structure and no real plan of action, so I set about designing one.

I immediately implemented a daily target and operational plan. The idea was to target specific officers based on complaints from citizens, and then develop a system to keep track of the investigations. I then designed an integrity-testing manual using my daughter's computer.

Testing and investigating police officers was much easier than working narcotics. I'd been around cops all my life; I knew their habits and most of all their mindset. There are three things that most get police officers in trouble: overtime, women, and trying to game the system rather than working.

However, as I learned later, as easy as it was to catch a police officer doing something wrong, doing something about it was an entirely different ballgame.

One of our first cases came from complaints that officers were stealing pornographic DVDs from vendors at Lexington Market.

First we checked evidence control to see if any porn DVDs had been submitted.

Nothing.

Then we set up a simple sting. I purchased $60 worth of porn tapes, put them in a duffel bag, and placed them on one of the suspected officers' post. Next we set up surveillance and called 911, reporting that the duffel bag was sitting on a sidewalk unattended.

When the officer arrived on the scene, he picked up the duffel bag and put it in the trunk of his car.

Next we checked evidence control to see if the officer had submitted the tapes into evidence during his shift. After we learned that he had not turned in the tapes, we continued surveillance on the officer.

When his shift was over, the officer left district headquarters with the duffel bag we had placed on the sidewalk. He took the bag and put it in the trunk of his private vehicle. After we observed him taking the tapes, we approached the officer, identified ourselves, and turned him in to his commanding officer to be disciplined.

One of the most common complaints we received in IID was officers planting drugs on suspects. Frankly, as the pressure in the city grew for the police to make more arrests, it didn't surprise me that officers would try to manufacture cases to make their numbers.

Let's remember that by the middle part of the past decade commanders began using arrest quotas to evaluate officers — the most backward thinking I have ever encountered as a police officer.

As a result, complaints about false arrests grew. And the sting that we designed to address the growing problem would forever change my career — not to mention rocking the city to its core.

I'll never forget the day we spent at headquarters on Labor Day 2000, stuffing Ivory Soap into plastic Ziploc bags. The idea was to be working when people least expect it. And setting up a sting on Labor Day was the best way to make sure no one got wind of it in advance.

We set up the operation on the 400 block of West Lafayette Avenue. Placing seven Ziploc bags filled with Ivory Soap on the park bench, I directed my squad to set up covert surveillance posts around the block.

As we set up our surveillance, I remember thinking how unfortunate it was we had to run this sting without video cameras. All of the IID cameras had been handed over to the Technical Assistance Reporting Unit, which had been set up by another New York transplant, Chief John Pignataro, to assist other tactical units with video surveillance.

I remember arguing with both the IID commander and my immediate supervisor that we needed the equipment, but to no avail. Thus we were forced to use still-cameras for a sting that would change the course of police corruption in the City of Baltimore forever.

Shortly after we set up surveillance, we made a 911 call to report seven bags of cocaine on a bench at St. Katherine's Memorial Park on Presstman Street.

An officer named Brian Sewell (no relation to me) responded. As we watched, he picked up the cocaine and placed it in his squad car and left the scene.

Let me note here that after the case became public both Sewell's lawyers and the media said another officer accompanying Sewell picked up the bags of soap. This is not true; I witnessed it myself.

After the evidence was picked up, we waited, keeping tabs on evidence control to see if the fake cocaine had been turned in.

Truthfully I didn't think this particular sting would be successful. Placing the cocaine on a bench in broad daylight was bound to look suspicious. My initial thought was that Officer Sewell would more than likely figure out the cocaine was fake and dispose of it.

At first that's exactly what appeared to have happened. The fake cocaine didn't show up in evidence control for several weeks. But then one of my detectives discovered drug charges against an 18-year old

African-American teen involving seven bags of crack cocaine from the same neighborhood.

We pulled the evidence tied to the case, and sure enough, they were our seven bags of Ivory Soap. We later learned that Sewell had picked up the fake cocaine, driven around the corner, and charged the teen with placing the seven bags on the park bench.

Let me say this: One thing I consistently find troubling and tiring is the idea that racism does not exist. Particularly when I have, through my own first-hand experience as a police officer, witnessed the false prosecution and persecution of young African-American men.

This case is a perfect example.

If we had not uncovered what Officer Sewell had done, this young man's life would have been over before it began. He would have spent years in jail; at the very least, he would be living with the lifelong consequences of a felony conviction. Unlikely to get a job, unable to access federal student aid for college, he would be permanently cut off from access to all the resources that could provide a young man hope and opportunity.

And the question has to be asked, Do you honestly think this is the first time a city police officer has planted drugs on a black man? Do you think this is the first time that a young African-American man has been falsely charged or falsely accused of a crime? I only ask that you consider the ramifications of what Officer Sewell did. He would have destroyed the life of a young man simply to get a stat. He set out to violate his oath as a police officer just to make a drug arrest.

And think about it, what would have happened to that young man? He would have become an outcast, a so-called "thug," a menace to society, an irredeemable criminal, a lifelong loser.

And if you still don't think that the corrosive legacy of racism still infects Baltimore, then just keep reading.

Sewell was suspended. The city state's attorney began investigating. Even Commissioner Ed Norris used the case as proof that corruption still existed in the Police Department and that he was going to root it out. Soon Sewell was indicted for perjury and misconduct. It was an open and shut case.

The statement of probable cause submitted by Sewell declared that he had observed the suspect placing the bags of cocaine on the bench.

It was a lie — and a crime.

But a funny thing happened along the way. Slowly but surely the case went from being about Officer Sewell's actions and more about mine. For the first time I began to realize that racism was not the exclusive domain of the Baltimore City Police Department, but systemic to the city, and most definitely a problem inside the prosecutor's office.

The prosecutor in the police misconduct unit who handled the case was a state's attorney I will not name. Early on in the case a staff member from her office warned me that she wanted to save Brian Sewell by discrediting me. I brushed it off at the time, but as the case progressed it became obvious that my source was correct.

From the beginning the prosecutor seemed unenthusiastic about the case. Often she would pepper me with questions about what she believed to be inconsistencies.

Then she started asking questions about the timeline we had created to match the photographs taken of Sewell picking up the fake narcotics. An officer from my squad created it, but she was sloppy, and used incorrect times.

So I fixed it. Removing the surveillance photographs from the timeline board, I created a new board with the correct times, shredded the old timeline, and submitted it. Remember, the timeline itself was not the evidence, it was simply a prop or guide.

But several days after I did this I picked up the Baltimore Sun to see my shredding of the timeline on the front page. In my mind, it was all part of a concerted campaign to discredit the charges against Officer Sewell. The only person in the State's Attorney's Office who knew I shredded the faulty timeline was — guess who? — the prosecutor I had been warned would try to discredit me.

The state eventually dropped the charges against Officer Sewell, citing lack of evidence, a move which touched off a firestorm of criticism. Commissioner Norris was angry, and then-Mayor O'Malley got into a very controversial spat with the city state's attorney, Patricia Jessamy, publicly admonishing her.

"She doesn't even have the goddamn guts to get off her ass and go in and try this case, and I'm tired of it," O'Malley said in an interview.

"If she doesn't have respect for the police, if she doesn't have respect for the people of this city, maybe she should get the hell out and let somebody else in who's not afraid to do the goddamn job."

His remarks sparked outrage, particularly among black leaders. Truthfully I think he was right, even though he could have been more diplomatic about it. Brian Sewell should have been prosecuted.

A decade later, Patricia Jessamy would lose her post to a white male opponent in the election of 2010, which centered on her lack of determination and failure to prosecute obviously guilty offenders. Gregg Bernstein, the new top city prosecutor, was elected largely by African-Americans fed up with Jessamy's laxity in prosecuting criminals.

Meanwhile, as the controversy over the Sewell case was heating up, I was having problems with one of the officers in my squad, problems that would further muddle the case against Brian Sewell.

A detective in my squad I'll call "John" was a good police officer, and a good friend. But his personal life was a mess. Like I said before, police officers are suckers for overtime and women — and female police officers especially. Add in a woman who is a stripper, and you have serious problems.

Put simply, John fell in love with a stripper who danced on The Block, Baltimore's red-light district which is located just a hundred yards down the street from police headquarters.

He left his wife, kids, home, boat, and all other worldly possessions to move in with her. He was head over heels in love, and it was driving him crazy.

He didn't trust her, so he would leave work early to meet her when she left work at the club. Then the next day he would show up late on the job. This was indeed a big change for John, who had always been a conscientious worker who showed up early and worked late.

Then late one night I got a phone call from him. He was crying. He needed to move out of the stripper's house.

Since he was broke, some of us cops moved him into a shed on the grounds of an off-site facility in Baltimore County where we store Internal Affairs case files.

It was a temporary arrangement for John, because he literally had no place else to go.

A few weeks later I got a call from the lieutenant that John was involved in a domestic dispute. I learned later he had discovered the stripper was pregnant by another man. In a rage, he destroyed her home. So I had to suspend him the next day.

But things got worse. Much worse.

On December 24th I got a call from a fellow sergeant in Internal Affairs: there had been a burglary at the off-site storage facility.

My first thought was John, did he have something to do with it?

When I arrived, several Baltimore County detectives were already on the scene. As I walked into the facility I couldn't believe my eyes.

Papers were thrown all over the floor, files were missing, the whole facility was in disarray. Upstairs on the second floor, where my office was located, I found my desk turned over, my computer on the floor, and my files missing, files that documented crimes committed by Baltimore City police officers.

I immediately suspected the burglary was an inside job. The alarm was deactivated, the code known only to me and the officers in my squad. If somebody had triggered the alarm, either my pager or the lieutenant's would have gone off.

Of course, all signs pointed to John. As the investigation proceeded, we learned that he was not only sleeping at the off-site, but he was bringing back women, mostly strippers, and having sex with them in the office.

Under questioning, he admitted he had staged the burglary to cover up his escapades with women and to vent his frustration over being suspended.

One of the detectives assigned to the case was a homicide sergeant I'll call "Mike." I had never worked with Mike before, but it seemed by his behavior that he suspected me. In fact, during the investigation it seemed he was focused almost entirely on me.

Shortly after the burglary my entire squad was ordered to take a lie detector test. It was a stressful time for everyone. We had all worked so hard — and, we believed, effectively. And now we were all suspects. I'll never forget the day after the first series of tests, one of my female detectives crying as she described the ordeal to her husband.

My test was administered by a Baltimore City Police lieutenant and an FBI agent. After the test I was escorted into a room and told I had passed. But this is the point where things turned weird.

Two days later I was asked to take the lie detector test again. I agreed.

When I arrived at the FBI offices I noticed immediately the set-up was quite different from the first test.

The test was administered in a different room. The examiner didn't ask many questions, just stared at me. When he was finished, he left the room.

I was being set-up.

One of the things I learned early on in the department is that many white officers assume black officers are stupid. That we don't know the rules, that we're not familiar with proper procedure, that we're incapable of picking up anomalies in the process.

So when he returned and said I failed, I wasn't having any of it.

Let me say right now I have never committed a crime in my entire life. And the idea that I would burglarize my own office is absurd; what was my motive?

But I was also familiar with the Baltimore City Police Administrative Manual, which stated that after a lie detector test an examiner should present the results to the person being tested. The examiner is not allowed to leave the room, otherwise they could return with someone else's result and the test would be invalid.

So after he said I failed, I told him he had administered the test incorrectly. He did not answer, and I left the office.

When I returned to my office I told my lieutenant about the results, at which point I was transferred out of my squad and into the branch of Internal Affairs that handles complaints for residents.

It was a bittersweet moment for me, to say the least. Eventually Mike's investigation concluded that it was indeed John who had burglarized the off-site building. But it didn't matter — I believe the opportunity that then-Commissioner Norris had given us was lost. Nor did it stop Mike from telling people in the department that he suspected I was responsible.

During the 10 short months of my work in the Internal Investigations Division, we had accumulated several dozen failures to report or turn over evidence; officers stealing money, having sex with prostitutes, and planting drugs on suspects. However as famed NYPD undercover Officer Frank Serpico once said: There is no such thing as a crooked cop.

There was a Greek police officer who was gambling on duty, was being paid-out by the store owner, and who ignored a signal 13 call — officer in trouble — as he sat at a video poker machine while he was under surveillance by us.

There was Lt. John Snow who robbed several banks using his service revolver while on duty. Both Snow and the Greek officer still got their full pension, even though they both had at least a year until retirement and had both committed crimes. From what I hear Snow's father collects his son's pension and puts the money into Snow's prison commissary account.

He's still in jail.

But there is something even more significant about what occurred.

A police department cannot function without integrity. If corrupt officers are allowed to remain on the force, their habits and bad practices spread like cancer. When the Brian Sewell case fell apart and State's Attorney Jessamy failed to prosecute, crooked officers took note.

And let me say this: I don't think John burglarized that off-site office to cover his tracks. I don't know for sure what happened or why he did it, but it was conveniently timed, and used as an excuse to dismiss dozens of cases against officers who do not deserve to wear a badge, a pattern of misdirection that will surface years later — I have no doubt — with even more damaging results.

CHAPTER SEVEN

The New York Boys

As I wrote in the previous chapters, when Ed Norris arrived in the Baltimore City Police Department, things changed, and fast.

The "New York Boys," as they were called, came to Baltimore with an entirely different style of policing, a philosophy of law enforcement developed in the Big Apple that was both highly tactical and aggressive. And our new Mayor Martin O'Malley, who staked his political future on lowering the homicide rate, embraced it.

The New York Boys were best known for the strategy called "Zero Tolerance Arrest Policy," based in part on a theory first developed nearly 30 years ago by social scientists George L. Kelling and James Q. Wilson called "Broken Windows," later expanded by criminologists Kelling and Catharine Coles in a landmark study titled "Fixing Broken Windows" in 1996.

The theory likened high crime areas to a dilapidated building with broken windows: If you don't fix the broken windows, vandals are more likely to break even more of them. To reduce crime, therefore, you fix the windows, which leads to arresting people for petty crimes. Arrest people for petty crimes, the theory goes, and the neighborhood improves.

Part of that strategy was to use the threat of mass arrests as an intelligence-gathering tool, a way to, in my opinion, shake down the neighborhood.

It's an idea that sounds good in theory, but when you boil it down, it leads to subtle change in the basic philosophy of policing that can create just as many problems as it solves.

In general, the primary function of a police officer is to arrest people who break the law, by either witnessing a crime or investigating it. But both Broken Windows and Zero Tolerance turned that whole idea on its head.

We were not just supposed to simply stop crime and arrest criminals: we were tasked with preventing crime. Our job switched from being a reactive force to being proactive. And with that change in philosophy, the way we functioned as police officers also changed.

You might ask, why would a strategy to arrest people for petty crimes prompt a change in the philosophy of policing, and who cares if it does?

The answer is simple.

A change in approach for a cop is almost always followed by a change in mentality. And when someone tells you to go out and be disruptive, to use your police powers as a blunt-force tool to create upheaval, the mentality of how you do your job changes as well.

I got a front row seat on just how this change in attitude can shape a police force and alter the mindset of officers when I was transferred to the Tactical Section Motorized Enforcement Team (M.E.T.) Unit.

The unit was set up by Commissioner Norris to create what is called "Omni-Presence" in high-crime areas. Put simply: a cop on every corner. I actually think it was one of the best units and best ideas that the New York people brought to Baltimore.

But at our first roll call, Norris gave us some unusual marching orders.

"Your job is to go out on the streets of Baltimore and harass the hell out of people," he said.

Immediately I turned to my squad and said that we weren't going to be harassing anyone. Yes, I was in a sense contravening an order, but as I explained, what he wanted us to do was not as simple as it seemed.

The Baltimore Sun picked up Norris's comments, which were pretty controversial and caused quite a media stir. But Norris was unperturbed; he returned to roll call the next night defiant.

"Sometimes when I say things the words find their way to the newspapers. So let me make it very clear to everyone here in case you did not understand me the first time. I want you to go out there and harass the hell out of people, do you understand me?"

The young officers responded: "Yes sir."

After Norris gave that order, I was worried that what would come out of it would be a bunch of citizen complaints. So I worked hard with my unit to make sure we followed the law.

Truthfully, even with that order we did do good work. I remember one day I was working in the Northwestern District with the M.E.T. Unit when a bunch of old ladies stopped me on their way to church.

They said they were glad to see so much police presence in the neighborhood because the drug dealers were so aggressive and hostile. I remember saying, "If you can't live in peace in your own neighborhoods, then we (the police) are going to make it so that they (the drug dealers) don't live in peace as well."

But they also said they were worried because the officers were aggressive with everyone in the neighborhood, not just the drug dealers.

I remember thinking to myself, this could get ugly.

The M.E.T. Unit was effective in part because Norris was a good leader, and he was smart. For one thing, he put us all in uniform so that our presence in the neighborhood was distinct and noticeable. He also held officers accountable, and was fair, so even though his marching orders were broad and potentially dangerous, he knew how to keep cops in line.

But the M.E.T. Unit experiment would also set a bad precedent. Norris unwittingly unleashed an operational culture that would become an entirely different animal under different leadership.

M.E.T. units would later evolve into plainclothes tactical squads, groups of officers who would drive around the city in unmarked cars with the intention only to disrupt. As Norris always said, the aggressive phase of the operation was supposed to be temporary, followed by investigations and arrests of the most violent and dangerous criminals in the area. But eventually, disruption became a way of life for certain units, a means to a very ugly end, and like the infamous Southwestern District Flex Squad — which was disbanded after one its members was accused of raping a suspect — this way of operating came with lots of serious problems.

Let me give you an example of how this culture of proactive policing could affect the thinking of young officers and lead them onto a path of bad habits.

One day I was riding in an unmarked car in the 3000 block of Preston Street with Officer Steve Rose. He wanted to join the DEA and get into narcotics in the worst way. He was impressed with my drug enforcement career and was seeking advice, hoping I could help him.

As we were driving, he pointed to a group of young men standing on the corner of an alley.

"Sarge, let me see how sharp you are," he said. "I bet, out of all those guys standing in the alley, you can't tell me who has drugs on him and who doesn't."

I replied, "You see that guy standing near the wall with the blue jeans on and the yellow shirt looking in our direction, but not really looking at us?"

"Yes," Steve answered.

"He's got drugs on him," I said.

But before I could say another word, Steve jumped out of the car and ran up to the young man I pointed out and began searching him. I couldn't believe it.

I got out of the car and slowly walked toward Steve. He was smiling proudly, he found 19 vials of crack cocaine on the suspect — but there was one problem, Steve had broken the law.

"Now tell me, what kind of probable cause you had in order to write a statement of charges to justify what you just did," I said.

Steve looked dumbfounded; he didn't have an answer. So I told Steve to get the young man's information and let him go.

The question I asked myself after that incident was, How in the world did a police officer make it through the Academy not knowing the basis of probable cause? Who taught him that you could simply walk up to any person on the corner and search them without the legal authority to do so?

The next day at roll call I made it clear to all my officers that you could not stop someone without probable cause.

"Always write what you see and never write anything you don't see," I emphasized. "Isn't that right, Officer Rose?"

Steve replied, "Yes sir."

Now you might be wondering why I would care about probable cause when the kid had drugs on him anyway? But isn't that just the type of technicality that lets criminals off the hook?

Let me say this: Police have power, a tremendous amount of power. They can arrest you, charge you, take away your freedom, and in some cases your property; and even take your life if they believe you are a dangerous threat.

This type of power, when abused, is the most socially destructive force you can imagine.

The law was designed to protect all of us from abuse of power, and it also makes a lot of sense. Having a reason to stop a person not only ensures that police do not use their powers to harass people, but it also encourages good and thorough police work, the type of work that can hold up in court.

Running up on a corner might seem like a good and effective way to get drug dealers off the street, but it has many potentially unintended consequences. What about the kid who is just standing there, a kid with a future who gets swept up and illegally arrested? His life may be over.

And of course, it's easier to view this with a jaundiced eye if you're not poor and black. If police started running up on corners in suburban neighborhoods, what do you think would happen? And do you think that kids are using, selling, and dealing drugs in suburban neighborhoods?

My point is that from what I've witnessed, the whole idea of disruptive, aggressive policing only makes matters worse, it floods the courts with flimsy cases, and it creates even more hostility between police and the community. And worse, it changes the idea of what it means to be a police officer.

Even in the worst neighborhoods police are supposed to represent and embody the law. We're police not just because we carry a gun and badge, but because we follow and uphold the law. Without it, we're nothing more than thugs, just like the criminal element but with even more power and resources.

I can't emphasize this enough. For when the Baltimore City Police Department started to arrest almost everybody — close to 100,000 people per year — it became crystal clear why this idea is so important.

CHAPTER EIGHT

Investigations In An Unreal City

Everyone has their own idea of what it means to be a criminal investigator, most of which comes from watching television.

On television the job of an investigator appears to be pretty procedural. You pore over forensic evidence, interview witnesses, and accumulate notes to re-create a narrative of a crime. Everything fits together like a puzzle. In the end, it's all pretty neat. The clues add up, the perpetrator has a complex motive that eventually reveals itself, and cops all try to outwork each other to see who can push the hardest.

Of course, I'm oversimplifying here; I'm not a television critic and it's easy to spout off on why television crime dramas are inaccurate and oftentimes unrealistic. But it's important to understand that the key to being a good investigator is having a feel for something that's a little more intangible: How the foibles of human nature play out in the environment where the crime occurs.

First of all, the streets of Baltimore's poorest neighborhoods are utter chaos. It's really hard to understand unless you've seen it yourself. Decades of poverty followed by unrelenting violence and finally the aforementioned presence of a "disruptive" police force have created a hardened community with a sense of distrust of not only police, but any outside authority or agency.

So when someone gets shot, you can do all the crime-lab work you want but you aren't going to get anywhere unless you have a feel for how the people think, live, and why they kill in inner city Baltimore.

Nowhere did this become more evident than when I worked as a shooting detective.

The opportunity to work shootings arose in 2001. I was still in the M.E.T. Unit, but the complaints were rolling in and I was starting to question the whole idea of the unit. Also, as an African-American I didn't like the fact that predominantly black neighborhoods were bearing the brunt of this new style of policing.

That's why when I bumped into Maj. Gregory Eades in Eastern District station and he offered me the chance to work shootings as a detective in the Eastern District, it only took me a couple of days to decide I wanted the job.

It was an exciting opportunity. Shootings are nothing more than failed homicides, so solving a shooting is a way police can actually prevent a killing. Not by disrupting, not by breaking the law, but actually solving a serious crime and taking a potential killer off the streets.

But the key to solving shootings is knowing how people in the community think, and applying what you know to get them to talk.

Take the case of one of my first shooting investigations.

A man had been shot on the corner of East Preston and Caroline Streets. We had one witness, a woman who told me she had seen the shooting, but when I asked her to come to headquarters to give a statement she said no.

Now the reason for this is quite simple: just after a shooting on a block known for drug dealing, people are paying attention, sometimes the people who did the shooting. So instead of forcing her into a police car and taking her downtown, I let her be, and hatched a plan.

The next day I returned to the neighborhood. I knew this woman, she was a drug addict, and she would be out on the street.

Sure enough, when I parked at the end of the block, she was out on the corner.

But instead of riding up on the corner and taking her in my car, I called a patrol officer and told him to arrest her for loitering. Then I ordered the officer to meet me at the Eastern District station with the witness.

There were two ideas behind this plan. First, if anyone in the neighborhood saw me or any other police officer talking to her or putting her in a vehicle without some sort of pretense, the word would get around that she was a snitch.

Second, I wanted her to be receptive to talking to me. Once she was under arrest, it was easy for her to justify talking, and I could offer to clear the arrest up if she was helpful.

When she arrived, I feigned a surprised look.

"What are you doing here?" I asked.

"I got arrested for loitering," she replied.

"Let me talk to her before you book her," I told the officer who had helped me pick her up.

I brought her back to the interview room and she told me everything about the shooting, enough to swear out an arrest warrant and close the case. During the interview I never mentioned the loitering charges. I drove her home myself later that day thinking, people will tell on anybody to stay out of jail, even their own grandmother.

One of the skills you have to develop pretty quickly if you're investigating shootings is the ability to know when someone is lying.

One strategy for lying in Baltimore City is simply to act like you didn't hear the question. I guess you could call it practiced disinterest. For example, you ask a simple question, like "What is your name?" and the witness or suspect will reply with a "Huh?" like they didn't even hear what you said. I believe it's a nervous reaction, a reaction that often means people are lying.

So I came up with a simple, almost comical way to counteract it, a strategy you won't see on many cop shows, unless you're watching a comedy.

For example, when I ask a question, and the witness or suspect replies "Huh?" I respond with a "Huh?"

Sergeant Sewell: "What's your name?

Witness: "Huh?"

Sergeant Sewell: "Huh?"

Witness: "Thomas Smith."

I don't know how I stumbled upon this method, but it almost always works, and would continue to work for as long as I kept replying "Huh?" It's almost like it stimulates a psychological reflex in the person being interviewed.

In fact, it works so well that other detectives would laugh hysterically watching me obtain answer after answer from the person I was interviewing.

Of course, working shootings you always had to expect the unexpected — like an unusual case I had in 2002.

We got a call that a man who was shot in the leg was admitted to Johns Hopkins Hospital.

When we arrived at the hospital, I noticed something unusual: Even though he was wounded in the leg, his pants were in pristine condition. No holes — so I thought immediately that he was lying.

I asked him what had happened, and he told me he was taking the trash out when a man he didn't know, robbed him and then shot him in the leg.

The victim noticed I was looking at his pants.

"I changed my pants before I came to the hospital," he said.

I knew the victim was telling the truth, but he was doing so for the wrong reasons.

So I put a guard on him after he was wheeled into the operating room. Then I obtained a warrant to search his home.

When we arrived we did indeed find a pair of pants with a bullet hole. We also found a Smith & Wesson with a spent shell casing, along with a pretty big cache of drugs and money.

In the basement we found several kilos of cocaine drug paraphernalia and thousands in cash as well. The haul was so big we had to use plastic drums to transport all of it.

So why had he shot himself?

Simple. He had shot himself to make it appear to "business" associates he had been robbed of the drugs and money.

When we reported back to the major, he called the news media and told us to meet the victim-now-turned-suspect at the hospital.

Upon his release from Johns Hopkins, the news media was waiting, asking him questions. We put him in an unmarked car and took him back to Eastern District station, where he confessed to shooting himself in the leg, as well as to possession of the stash. The next day on television I remember watching the report on our case: "He went into the hospital a shooting victim, and left, a suspect."

Truth be told, my squad had a pretty high clearance rate, all pretty much the result of common sense and knowing the streets. The commander of the Eastern District, Major Eades, commended me for my work. "Word on the streets is when you shoot someone in our district they disappear," said the major, meaning we were making good arrests.

One day I accompanied the major to COMSTAT, the weekly meeting held at police headquarters to review crime statistics and spot trends, that "The Wire" portrayed as a formal way to humiliate people — which is pretty much true.

At our COMSTAT review, I recall Col. Robert Stanton, head of the city's Criminal Investigation Division, complimenting the major on how well we were doing.

"You guys are doing a terrific job," the colonel said. "You've closed all of your shooting cases thus far. Can you stand a review of your shooting cases?"

Major Eades stood on the podium with his chest out and stated: "Not only can we stand a review, colonel; we welcome a review."

Colonel Stanton then looked in my direction and stated, "You guys are costing me a lot of overtime. Good job Kelvin!"

The colonel was so pleased, he asked me to teach other detectives how to investigate shooting cases. And before I knew it, I was getting calls from other districts asking me if I could train additional officers.

But as usual inside the Baltimore Police Department — and I'm sure anywhere — when you succeed, there is always someone who is going to try to bring you down.

One night I responded to a call for a shooting in the Douglas Homes Housing Project. It turned out the victim had been shot in the Southeastern District, and ran four blocks into the Eastern District.

Of course, as I've already discussed, the emphasis on stats creates a strange sense of odd disincentives to being truthful about what really happens on the streets. This is nothing new, but the pressure on the BPD during the reign of Mayor O'Malley, who staked his entire political future on reducing crime, was unrelenting.

So I decided to respond because we had a white major from the Southeastern District who was notorious for convincing shooting victims they had been shot in the Eastern District.

I was able to interview the victim before he was transported to the hospital. He said he was at a cookout with his family at Douglas Homes, when a man he didn't know walked up and shot him, after which he ran the four blocks into the Eastern District.

I went to the hospital to inform the Southeastern District detectives that the shooing did not occur in the Eastern.

Once I turned the investigation over to Southeastern District detectives, they, along with the major entered the victim's hospital room and shut the door. A short time later, the Southeastern District commander walked out of the examination room and stated to me, "This is an Eastern District shooting. The Eastern's got this."

The major then looked in my direction and walked away with the Southeastern District detectives following behind him, smiling.

Several weeks later, another man was shot on Milton Avenue in the Southeastern District and ran into the Eastern District. Again, the Southeastern District commander showed up on the scene. But this time Major Eades was waiting for him.

Again the Southeastern District commander interviewed the victim and concluded that he had been shot in the Eastern District. But based on what the victim had told me — that he had been shot on Milton Avenue — Major Eades put an end to it real fast.

Southeastern was going to have to work the shooting. I'll never forget the look on the Southeastern District detectives' faces when they realized they were actually going to have to work.

But that didn't stop the commander from trying to get rid of the case. If he couldn't convince anyone about where the victim was shot, then why not try to convince the victim he wasn't shot at all?

If that sounds confusing, let me explain.

Later I got a call from Homicide Maj. Laurie Zuromski; the major was very upset.

"Kelvin, how could you have a man who was shot, transported to my Homicide office instead of the hospital?" she asked.

I told the major it wasn't our investigation. But I later learned the Southeastern District commander, when his first plan to rid his district of the case didn't work, had convinced the victim he was not shot at all, and had him transported down to Homicide for an interview.

But the tactic didn't work; it all came out in the wash at COM-STAT.

The major was then banned from showing up at shooting scenes. And later he was forced to retire after he was caught having sex in his office with another officer.

I guess he couldn't convince anyone that it happened in a different district commander's office?

So as you can see the emphasis on stats can lead to some very strange outcomes.

Still, I was proud of my work in the Eastern District. In 2002 we closed 90 percent of our cases, the highest percentage ever — a record that still stands.

CHAPTER NINE

Homicide: Death On The Streets

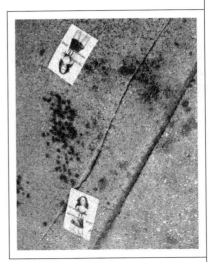

In February 2006 I arrived at my final and, in retrospect, most politically vexing assignment, Homicide.

Technically Homicide is the elite unit in the department, home to the purportedly most effective and seasoned investigators in the BPD.

But while Homicide had been portrayed as a crack squad on shows like "Homicide: Life on the Street" and "The Wire," when I arrived on the floor things were quite different.

Cronyism and the lure of almost limitless overtime, without, in my opinion, having to work to earn it, had made landing a position in the unit one of the most lucrative assignments in the department. Only detectives in some of the tactical units like VCID (Violent Crimes Impact Division) could take home the $60,000 to $70,000 per year in overtime pay that was typical for a homicide detective.

And since, as I have discussed earlier in this book, politics had altered the normal path of promotion inside the BPD by completely politicizing the command structure, the unit that used to be made up of 15- to 20-year veterans now had near rookies investigating major murder cases.

Even for people unfamiliar with policing it's not hard to understand why being a homicide detective would be the culmination of one's career, not the beginning.

A good homicide detective needs to have a breadth of knowledge of all the workings of the department, investigative procedures, and also a sense of the streets, to be effective — skills that are developed over time, a great deal of time. Now we had officers assigned to the unit with just two or three years on, neophyte rookies handling complex cases.

Things had gotten so bad that my first night on the floor, when the lieutenant in charge gave me a rundown on my squad, I was dumbfounded.

First he told me I had a detective in my squad who was afraid of the streets, a cop who would only go out in a car with smoked windows, which he would drive to the scene and not get out of. There was another detective who rarely solved cases because he felt "unmotivated."

"Kelvin, it's hard to get rid of these detectives. You're going to be dealing with more politics than cases up here."

Of course, as usual, Baltimore City's ongoing continuum of violence made pondering the politics of homicide a luxury.

In fact within a few hours of reporting to the floor I found myself standing on the grounds of the city's Douglas Homes Housing Project in East Baltimore, looking at a body.

The victim, a woman, was found lying in the street just outside the entrance of the city-run housing project a few blocks south of Johns Hopkins Hospital. Her throat slashed, she had bled out quickly, dying within minutes, literally drowning in her own blood.

Next to her body was the Maryland State identification card of a male who we later learned was the victim's boyfriend, and who several witnesses had spotted with her shortly before she was murdered.

I was pleased, my first homicide as a supervisor and we had a pretty good lead on a suspect. It was more luck than anything else, to be sure, but given the fact that Baltimore notches a homicide every 36 hours I was happy to take what was given and put the case down quickly.

Unfortunately, there was an obstacle to making an arrest I hadn't anticipated — a beach vacation.

Let me say this before I tell you what happened next. For all the heavily touted policing concepts, such as Zero Tolerance, that I have discussed in this book, in my mind the best way to prevent a future homicide is by solving the murders that have already occurred. Taking a murderer off the street, someone who has already killed, goes a long way toward disrupting the cycle of violence that rules the streets of Baltimore.

The same goes for shootings, which are of course failed homicides.

That's why what happened next is something that still troubles me to this day and I think goes a long way toward explaining why Baltimore continues to have one of the highest homicide rates in the country.

As I said before we had a pretty solid lead and a very likely suspect. The ID card and the witnesses, coupled with the fact that the day before, the victim had called police and accused the same man of assaulting her.

But as I stood over the body, the detective on the case (who I will not name) asked me a question, a sort of Welcome to Homicide inquiry.

"Sarge, I'm on vacation tomorrow for four days, I'm taking my family to the beach. I'll write the warrant for the suspect when I get back, okay?" the detective asked.

I couldn't believe what I was hearing. There I was standing over the body of a woman who had just been cut and bled like an animal while the man who did it was walking free, and the detective wanted me to hold the warrant so he could go to the beach? Was he serious?

So I told him right there on the scene in no uncertain terms that I wanted the warrant written that evening, an order that didn't sit well with him.

Within 24 hours the Warrant Apprehension Task Force had locked the suspect up.

So when I arrived back at the office I asked the lieutenant, "Is this how it's done down here? Detectives know who the suspect is and decide to write the warrant when they return from vacation? By that time, the suspect could kill again."

The lieutenant laughed: "Welcome to Homicide, Kelvin."

"Not in my squad," I answered.

At least that was my intention. But I soon discovered that the lieutenant was right, politics ruled in Homicide even more than narcotics and other coveted assignments, and getting people to work and be effective was sometimes nearly impossible.

Let me give you an example.

One day one of my best detectives, Mike Moran, had to travel to Hagerstown Correctional Center to pick up a witness. I knew the trip would take all day, so I told him to take one of the three Chevy Cavaliers assigned to the squad.

Of the three, the car with tinted windows was in the best shape, which isn't saying much. The vehicles were all circa mid-1990s and had more miles on them than a world atlas.

Still, the white Cavalier was in the best condition, and I didn't want Mike to get stuck on the highway halfway back from Hagerstown with a prisoner in the back seat.

After Mike left, the detective who I believe to this day was afraid of the streets showed up late for work.

I ordered him to go to the scene of a recent murder and knock on some doors to look for witnesses.

The detective left the office, returning a short time later.

"Sarge, have you seen the white Cavalier?"

I replied, "Oh, yeah, Mike had to drive the vehicle to Hagerstown. Here, take these keys," I said, throwing the detective a set of keys to another vehicle, without tinted windows. The detective looked at me and slowly walked away.

A few minutes later, I walked past the detective's desk and he was still sitting there.

"Why aren't you at the scene?" I asked.

"I'm just waiting for Mike to get back," he replied.

"Mike will be gone all day," I told him. "I need you to get on the streets now."

The detective then gave me a nervous look and walked out of the office.

A few minutes later, he reappeared at my door.

"Sarge, I'll just respond out to the area where my homicide occurred tomorrow, okay?"

"Not tomorrow. You better get on the street," I ordered. "Now."

This time, the detective shot me a glance that was more confrontational than nervous: He was clearly pissed off.

A couple of hours later, he reappeared again. "No one out there knew anything," he said.

I'd been involved in enough investigations to know that the detective was lying. If he had actually visited the scene and if he had actually knocked on doors he would have come up with something.

That's why we do it, that's why we get out of cars and pound the pavement. A neighborhood in Baltimore is like a universe unto itself, the people that live there all know what's going on and someone is always willing to talk if you're willing to ask and listen.

I complained to the lieutenant.

"I told you he was scared of the street," was all the lieutenant said.

Next I had to deal with another detective who was outright lying about interviewing witnesses.

He would write reports recounting interviews with witnesses who could not later be found at their listed addresses.

So I started backtracking and checking his work, a habit I developed after two of the detectives in my Eastern District shooting squad wrote a progress report stating that a person I had asked them to interview knew nothing about a case.

Unfortunately the address they listed for the witness was an abandoned home. Needless to say, I learned early on in my career that in the Baltimore City Police Department lying was routine, and if you wanted to be a successful supervisor you had to trust, but verify.

Thus when I had suspicions about one of my detectives in Homicide, I handled it the same way — I followed up.

I recall visiting the home of a supposed witness on the 2500 block of Garrett Avenue, in Waverly just north of East 25th Street. According to a report filed by the detective, he had spoken with the owner of the home who told him her son did not know anything about the case.

When I knocked on the door and asked her to confirm what she had told my detective, the same woman who answered the door looked dumbfounded. She didn't know what I was talking about. In fact, she told me she had never spoken to any police officers.

Over time, I accumulated six false reports by this detective, six incidents where he had simply made up the date, circumstance, times, and alleged statements of witnesses.

This type of behavior is so utterly damaging to the process of investigation and a slap in the face to the department and the people of the city, that I brought it to the attention of then-Col. Frederick Bealefeld, who would later become police commissioner.

Colonel Bealefeld listened patiently as I described the false reports and showed him the evidence of the detective's malfeasance. He shook my hand and told me I was doing a good job.

"I'm doing what you asked me to do," I recall telling him.

And then, nothing happened. The detective wasn't even disciplined. So I transferred him out of my squad, and today, that officer with little or no compunction about lying still sits on the Homicide floor, probably falsifying reports and collecting fat paychecks filled with overtime.

But that particular detective was just one of several slackers I had to deal with.

In 2007 one of my detectives had been working on the case of a victim known as Jay Rock for nearly three months.

I remember the day of the murder, we were standing next to the porch where the victim's body lay. There was a Coca-Cola can sitting on the stoop.

When the detective arrived shortly after me, he stood over the body and quipped, "I guess we have another who-done-it."

I took the detective aside. "Before you start making statements," I said sternly, "try and find out who did it first."

Let me explain why I did this.

Cops are notorious for cracking jokes and making off-color remarks over dead bodies, comments that can seem cavalier and even cruel given the circumstances. It's part stress-reliever, along with being a way of coping with the pressure of being constant close-up witnesses to the worst types of human behavior. That's why I don't really pay much attention when a patrol officer mouths off on the scene or says something inappropriate: I understand the stress of being a cop in Baltimore City.

But there's one exception to that rule, and that's a detective working Homicide.

There's only one person on the scene of a murder who is ultimately responsible for what happens to the investigation — the primary homicide detective.

He or she's the orchestrator and the administrator, the witness to all that occurs and the expert regarding everything that happened.

At Homicide, we set the tone.

Thus when the homicide detective arrives on the scene of a murder, he or she must be alert, be thinking, and most important, focused.

If the detective's standing around joking or making offhand remarks, or even speculating about the crime, than he or she is signaling to other people on the crime scene that he's not paying attention and really doesn't care.

And that sense of responsibility, or lack thereof, was one the biggest challenges I faced with my squad.

There used to be a saying on the floor, a standard line fed to the press, that's there's not a homicide detective on the floor who doesn't want to solve a murder.

Sounds nice, but it's lacking in accuracy. It goes without saying that we all wanted to solve the countless homicides that take place on the streets of the city, but were we actually willing to do the work to solve them?

Sometimes, not much.

During my career in the division I learned that for many detectives dead bodies meant dollars, overtime pay and lots of it, as I've said before. There were many cases when I believe a warrant was not immediately written or an arrest was not made to prolong an investigation, to allow a detective to make more overtime.

And so it was the same with the Jay Rock case.

Three months went by and the case was still open. In fact, according to the progress reports filed by the detective, he had yet to interview a single witness or find one piece of evidence.

So I decided to close the case myself to prove a point. Sometimes it's just better to lead by example, and I couldn't really think of a better opportunity to do so than an unsolved murder.

So when the detective took leave for his honeymoon, the first thing I did was visit the home of the victim's girlfriend, a seemingly obvious place to start.

Sure enough, the family told me she had been with Rock the day he was shot. So I took the girl down to Homicide for an interview.

At first she was uncooperative, but I took a chance and said I knew she was with Jay Rock when he was shot because we found her DNA on the soda can.

Honestly I was just fishing, but the gambit worked. She started to cry, admitting she was indeed with Rock, telling me she was not only with him but identifying his killer, a Blood gang member with the street name Munchie.

She not only gave me the suspect's name but a taped statement, and picked Munchie out of a photo array. Basically, I had solved the case in two days.

But I soon learned it was far from finished.

I brought what I had to my lieutenant for review. He laughed.

"You only have one witness, Kelvin. The State's Attorney's Office isn't going to accept this case or approve the warrant."

I was familiar with the debate over the informal one-witness rule that the State's Attorney's Office followed, but I honestly thought it was more posturing than reality. Basically the rule was, they would not prosecute a murder case with only a single witness, a rule that I always thought was arbitrary and absurd.

You prosecute based on the quality of evidence, not the quantity. Murderers don't adhere to procedures and are rarely considerate enough to make sure they have at least two witnesses before they shoot Pookie in the head.

But the lieutenant was firm, there was no point in bringing this case to prosecutors without a second witness.

So I hit the streets again, pounding the pavement where Jay Rock was gunned down. Luckily I found another witness who also gave me a taped statement and picked the suspect out of a photo array.

Three days and the case was closed, we had a suspect, and two witnesses to identify him.

But this wasn't the result of brilliant detective work, or even luck. It was simply a matter of caring enough to work, and understanding how to establish relationships with witnesses and build trust.

Still, there were more hoops yet for me to jump through.

Before I could write the warrant, the assistant state's attorney assigned to the case had to interview both witnesses twice. Thus I had to pick them up in the neighborhood and bring them to the prosecutor's office at a time convenient for the attorney, with little consideration by the prosecutor regarding how tricky and dangerous transporting homicide witnesses can be.

This process of repeatedly transporting witnesses, which happens all the time, is a perfect example of just how out of touch prosecutors had become in the Baltimore City State's Attorney's Office.

Solving the typical crime of violence in Baltimore relies less on forensics, or ballistics, or spectral analysis, or any of the other slickly produced techniques shown on television, than it does on witnesses.

To do my job, I need people to talk. And not just any people; I need the people who live with, and fear, the young men who commit the bulk of the violent crimes that keep this city in an unending state of chaos.

These people are poor, isolated, and scared. When they choose to step forward and give statements they are risking their lives, quite literally.

That's why going to pick them up over and over again is not only burdensome from an administrative point of view, but it puts the witness at risk every time I drive to the neighborhood, however covertly.

Oftentimes the witnesses live side by side with the friends, family, and fellow gang members of the person they have accused of committing the crime. The last thing they need is to be seen riding around with a cop. And believe me, even in an unmarked car everyone knows who we are.

And as much as then-Chief Prosecutor Patricia Jessamy and her public relations staff had made noise about the so-called "stop snitching" culture in Baltimore, from what I've seen behind the scenes, the way they handled witnesses did just as much to make life difficult for those people as any thug carrying a gun.

For those who haven't heard of the phrase "Stop Snitchin'" it first became part of the popular lexicon when a DVD made in Baltimore in 2004 was released featuring local drug dealers warning area residents not to talk to police. The video gained national attention, helped in part by a cameo appearance by NBA basketball star and former Baltimore resident Carmelo Anthony.

First let me say this about the whole culture of Stop Snitchin' and the way it was handled by the prosecutor's office and in part by police: They wanted us to believe that the idea people didn't want to talk was somehow new, or at least a recent development, a change in the cultural mindset of the city.

Now, I have been a police officer since 1987, and I've worked investigations for more than two decades. So for the record, don't let police commissioners fool you, or allow prosecutors to blow smoke with excuses about the so-called Stop Snitchin' mentality.

It's nothing more than a blame game.

Since the beginning, witnesses have been reluctant to talk. Even in the best neighborhoods people understand the risks of fingering a murderer. Never in my career has there been a time when anyone simply walked up to you on a crime scene and started telling you what happened — without a lot of coaxing.

It's not that it never happened — I suppose there must be occasional exceptions to the rule — but the truth is it rarely occurs now, just as it rarely did 20 years ago. So when you hear a prosecutor or police officer talk about Stop Snitchin' — don't buy it.

And since when did murderers not try to intimidate witnesses?

Seriously, our job is and always has been to get people to talk who don't want to. If it were easy, then everyone could do it.

The problem really is about the lack of connection between the police, prosecutors, and the community they serve.

The majority of the officers in Homicide are white. When I first took over my job four out of six detectives in my squad were white.

Now don't get me wrong, I'm not saying a white detective isn't just as capable as solving murders as an African-American. Mike Moran, who happens to be white, is one of the best detectives in the department, period.

But in order to get people to talk, and I mean the African-American residents who live in neighborhoods where the majority of murders occur, you have to both understand them and respect the issues and obstacles they're dealing with. In a sense, I'm talking about empathy.

Nobody trapped in a poor neighborhood is going to identify a Blood murderer unless you build a certain level of trust with that person.

So when prosecutors keep telephoning witnesses and badger them before the case even makes it to trial, it makes my job of keeping the witnesses cooperative even more difficult.

With the two witnesses for the Jay Rock case, the prosecutor asked a bizarre array of questions that left me scratching my head.

"Why are you doing this? Don't you know the Bloods can hurt you or kill you if they find out?" the prosecutor assigned to the case asked them both.

It seemed to me as if the prosecutor was trying to talk them out of being witnesses. Each time I would bring them down for another interview I would have to talk them down. I was so confused I asked the ASA the purpose for the line of questioning.

"Kelvin, my boss told us not to take on too many cases because the department doesn't want us to overload ourselves."

I couldn't believe what I was hearing. There were murderers walking the streets of the city and all Patricia Jessamy's office cared about was caseload! I knew enough prosecutors who came in at noon and left on sunny days by 3 p.m. to understand that overburdened attorneys was hardly the issue in that department.

And even after two trips to the prosecutor's office I had to bring the witnesses down again because the first prosecutor transferred the case to another attorney, standard practice in that office.

All the while these witnesses were more than likely facing intimidation and threats.

Meanwhile if they were hoping the Witness Protection Program could bail them out, think again. The entire budget in the prosecutor's office for the relocating of witnesses when I was working was roughly $500,000 per year. That's less than they spent on hiring people to write press releases and badmouth the Police Department, though an office full of spokespeople have since been let go following the 2010 election.

So while the case was shuffled around the State's Attorney's Office I had to bring the witnesses down to the Mitchell Courthouse three more times. Fortunately the case held together and Munchie pled guilty, receiving a 50-year sentence for the murder.

Still, even when I presented all the details of the case to my lieutenant, he said we could not move the detective who let the case languish for three months out of Homicide.

"That's politics," the lieutenant said.

But that's not the only type of politics inside the Homicide Unit that determines whose case gets solved and whose doesn't.

One day I was sitting in my office when I noticed almost all the detectives in my unit were getting ready to respond to a murder scene.

More than curious I confronted a detective who I'd never seen so excited about working a homicide case before.

"Sarge, we got a murder, a white lady was killed in Brooklyn," he said. "Come on, Sarge, we need the whole squad for this one."

It was not just him, my entire squad was getting ready to respond.

"We got a 'red ball' case," someone said.

A red ball case — also known as a "shitstorm" or "clusterfuck" — is a high profile case that draws political and media attention and is typically investigated by all detectives on a shift, as when someone influential and well-known, like City Councilman Ken Harris, is murdered, or a police officer is shot. In this case it was the color of the woman's skin that made it a red ball.

These were some of the same detectives who let murder cases of black men linger for months, but a white lady, that's a priority.

In fairness however I should note that red ball cases often make or break a detective's career.

But in the end we discovered the woman was not murdered at all; instead she died of natural causes.

Still, the behavior of the detectives that day, and on other cases as well, made me more than determined to change things up.

So I transferred three detectives out of my squad and brought in three new officers who I knew wanted to work hard and cared.

Meanwhile many of the detectives still in the squad would not talk to me — but I didn't care, I wanted to solve cases; and if they weren't going to help, I didn't have a problem with a little office tension.

Then once I got my squad in shape, things started to fall into place. And by 2007 I finally felt I had assembled a good group of detectives that I could trust would do their best.

The next four years in Homicide were some of the most interesting and troubling in my career.

I worked horrendous cases, and was involved with some of the most high profile murders in the city.

Eleven of those homicides have been recounted in the Case Files in the first half of this book.

About the Authors

STEPHEN JANIS is an award-winning reporter who publishes *Investigative Voice,* an online watchdog journalism website based in Baltimore Maryland. As a staff writer for the former *Baltimore Examiner* (and one of only a handful of reporters who worked at the paper for its entire existence) he won a Maryland-Delaware-DC Press Association award in 2008 for investigative reporting on the high rate of unsolved murders in Baltimore. In 2009 he won an MDDC Press Association award for Best Series for his articles on the murders of prostitutes.

As co-founder of the independent investigative website *Investigative Voice,* Janis's work uncovering corruption and government waste in Baltimore City will be chronicled in the upcoming national documentary "Fit To Print."

The site has won worldwide critical acclaim for its unconventional presentation and hardnosed reporting and is read regularly by insiders in city government as well as the police department.

Janis is the author of two novels, Orange: *The Diary of an Urban Surrealist* and *This Dream Called Death.* In addition to reporting and directing content for *Investigative Voice* he currently teaches journalism at Towson University.

KELVIN SEWELL is a 22-year veteran of the Baltimore City Police Department. A former narcotics officer tasked to the U.S. Drug Enforcement Administration, he worked on major drug investigations for nearly a decade, later becoming a supervisor in the BPD's Internal Affairs Division, where he led several high profile integrity operations.

Sewell worked as a supervisor and investigator in the fabled Baltimore City Homicide Unit, working some of the most notorious cases in one of the most violent cities in the country. He attended Harvard Associates Forensic Science School and received a Bachelor of Arts Degree in criminology from Coppin State University.

Following his retirement as a Baltimore homicide detective he took a job as Lieutenant in the Pocomoke City Police Department on Maryland's lower Eastern Shore, where he currently continues to serve.

STEPHEN JANIS/Photographed by Taya Graham

Made in the USA
Middletown, DE
12 February 2018